To:
Jason &
Lesley

Merry Christmas

Remembering why
we celebrate this
Holiday through
reading and walking
through this little
book ~ I know I
loved it !!

Momma (G.)

1

Sincerely,

Jesus

Sincerely, Jesus

Edward Goble

Shaken Books

Revised 01292012

Unless otherwise indicated, Scripture references are from The Holy Bible: New King James Version (NKJV) Copyright © 1982 by Thomas Nelson, Inc.

Scripture references marked NIV are from The Holy Bible: New International Version (NIV) Copyright © 1973, 1978, 1984 by International Bible Society

Scripture references marked NLT are from The Holy Bible: New Living Translation (NLT) Copyright © 1996, 2004 by Tyndale Charitable Trust. Used by permission of Tyndale House Publishers.

Scripture references marked KJV are from The Holy Bible: King James Version

For more information contact:
Shaken Books
PO Box 442
Campbellsville, KY 42719
office@shakenbooks.com

ISBN-13: 978-1469996929
ISBN-10: 1469996928

Cover Design by Meghan McDonald-Gale
Interior Design by Bluegrass Creative

Table of Contents

Introduction - You've Got Mail

My wife just returned from her daily walk down the gravel drive to retrieve today's mail. MaryAnn would never admit it but she loves to be the one who gets the mail. I do, too, actually. Not to be dramatic, but it's a little like Christmas morning with that moment of anticipation when you get to the creaky grey box, unsure of the treasure it may hold. That little hinged door is like the ribbon on a Christmas package. I guess that's a stretch, but you know what I mean. You just don't know what might be inside, it could be something wonderful!

I'm not sure why the old mailbox still carries the mystique it once did; it seems like all we receive anymore are bills we don't want and advertisements for things we can't afford or don't need. That wasn't always the case. Some of us remember the days when we used to receive real letters in the mail. Actual hand-scribed treasures from a loved one who set aside time to sit down and write. So, we ruffle through all the ads and bills and notices hoping, subconsciously, to find something real. Maybe it's that memory, or something like it, that drives us to want to be the one who gets the mail.

In many ways, today's communication technology is far superior to the old first-class letter. It's instant, for one thing. Nowadays, to reach a loved one, you don't have to drop your letter in an impersonal blue box and wonder when and if it will arrive. You simply email, IM, or call their cell phone - instant communication. Technology has brought people closer together than ever and rendered nearly obsolete the time-honored, saliva-sealed, postage-paid traditional letter. This is sad because email, Instant Messaging, video conferencing and cell phones are great for business, terrific for touching base, but, when it comes to deep, thoughtful communication, there is nothing quite like the hand-written page or face-to-face talk. We have exchanged real and deep for quick and nimble. Morphed from talking, writing and listening to texting, emailing and chatting, usually while simultaneously downloading, surfing and gaming.

Life has become so fast, instant and multi-task oriented, that, if we're not doing a dozen things and running late for a few appointments, we begin to feel like we're slacking. There is almost nothing left that grabs us, captures our imagination and attention and forces us to stop and take notice. Personal letters still do that. They do for me at least.

Imagine getter personal letter from Jesus. Now that would get your attention.

What if tomorrow, mixed in among the bills, notices and bargain flyers in your mailbox, was a letter from Jesus. First, you might think it was kind of spooky since Jesus hasn't been on earth for a couple thousand years (probably justifiable spookiness at most levels). But it would certainly get your attention. Think of how a letter from Jesus would have captured the attention of seven churches in Asia Minor. Like you, they might have been puzzled to receive such a letter, because, by this time, Jesus had been in heaven for some forty or fifty years since His resurrection and ascension. And, since we know that Jesus is in heaven, sitting at the right hand of His

Father, whether it's three weeks, four decades or two thousand years, a personal letter from Him is just something you don't expect to see.

But Jesus had some things to say to His church, even from heaven, so He found an old friend, the apostle John, who was presently in exile on the Island of Patmos, and dictated the letters with the understanding that John would deliver them, or have them delivered, to the churches.

If you think it would be strange to find a letter from Jesus in your mailbox, you might have an idea what those young leaders were feeling as they opened the note addressed personally to them.

What would you be thinking? "Yikes! Why me?" They say that your life flashes before your eyes when you are in the midst of some tragic or life-threatening experience. A letter from heaven would probably trigger a similar phenomena, all the behavior I had tried to forget, all the things I had done in secret, all my mistakes come rushing back as I imagine what He might be writing about.

A letter from Jesus would be a letter that I would read over and over again, put under my pillow to read before going to sleep and upon waking in the morning. I would want to know every detail of what Jesus was thinking, every nuance of what He was asking of me, and I would want to respond, to go or change or whatever He wanted. I would want to make Him proud, to make it right, to honor His request.

When Jesus says "church"

In Revelation chapters two and three, we find seven letters addressed to seven churches spread across Asia Minor. The common understanding would be that Jesus was writing to those specific churches and that the word He gives is exclusively for them. But, that isn't necessarily the case, beginning with our understanding of the word "church." Resist the typical definition of a building with a cross or a steeple and a big parking lot and education wing. When we say church, we suggest the facility. We "go to Church." We meet each other "at the church." And to remove any doubt as to the definition, we put big signs in front of our meeting places that identify them as being the "church." But, if that is the picture you get when you hear Jesus use the word "church," you'll be inclined to miss much of what He says. Because, when Jesus says "church," He isn't talking about a building - He's talking about people.

The only sense in which the church is understood as a building is through the use of a word picture where people with different gifts and abilities serve in various roles and functions. For example, the apostles' teaching is the foundation, and Jesus Christ is the chief cornerstone of the structure. Other word pictures are employed by New Testament writers, as well, such as a body where Christ is the head; a flock over whom Jesus is the Good Shepherd; and a priesthood where Jesus is Chief Priest - all images of this innumerable group of people, spanning centuries and continents, called the church. When Jesus addresses a letter to the church in Ephesus, He is writing to the Christian people in that community, not the facilities in which they met.

So, first of all, these seven letters were meant for the people gathered in Christ's name in the city to which the letter is addressed: Ephesus, Smyrna, Pergamos, Thyatira, Sardis, Philadelphia and Laodicea. Seven cities scattered around Asia Minor who had known a Christian presence for a couple of decades, a result of the dispersion of the church out of Jerusalem and the ministry of Paul in Ephesus. But then Jesus does a peculiar thing. He ends each letter by expanding its contents to all of us, saying,

"He who has an ear, let him hear what the Spirit says to the churches."

Loosely paraphrased, this could be, "Some or all of this may apply to you as well, so listen closely to what the Holy Spirit may be saying to you." Notice He writes, "He who has an ear, let him hear..." now that's not speaking exclusively of men (he), but of people. Individual Christians are supposed to be "listening" to what the Spirit is saying.

He has a message for seven groups of actual, local, historical people, and in addition, He instructs christian people, individually and corporately, through the ages of the church, to learn from each letter as well.

Scripture is amazing like that. The letters, visions and prophetic messages of the Bible are all written in a certain historical context, but with the touch of God's Spirit, obscure verses from little read books can prick our heart in ways that are intensely personal. The apostle Paul pointed this out when he wrote:

All Scripture is given by inspiration of God, and is profitable for doctrine, for reproof, for correction, for instruction in righteousness, that the man of God

may be complete, thoroughly equipped for every good work. 2 Timothy 3:16-17

"*All* Scripture." So, even though these seven letters were dictated by the Risen Lord to His dear friend John over 1900 years ago, written to seven churches around Asia Minor, they applied in ways the Holy Spirit would define to the other churches around Asia at that time as well. Not only that, they hold application for churches of the renaissance, Christians meeting together in the Old West, and Christians scattered throughout the world in the twenty-first century. These seven letters are from Jesus to the whole church. To me and to you.

He has more for you

As you read these letters from Jesus with an open and expectant heart, ready to listen and respond to the word of Christ, the Holy Spirit will make each letter alive, powerful and personal. He will speak to areas of your life that you didn't think He saw, or didn't know He cared about. It will be a time of introspection and a time of change, because He loves you so much that He doesn't want to leave you the way you are. He has more for you, more depth, more wholeness, more of Himself to share.

Though the letters are not signed in the traditional sense (the Author identifies Himself at the beginning of each), I can vividly imagine the Author, having considered every word and every reader, knowing the depth of truth and the promise of life that each letter contains, would want each person through the ages to know that it was written especially for *you*.

Written truly, genuinely, sincerely Jesus.

To the angel of the church of Ephesus write,

These things says He who holds the seven stars in His right hand, who walks in the midst of the seven golden lampstands: "I know your works, your labor, your patience, and that you cannot bear those who are evil. And you have tested those who say they are apostles and are not, and have found them liars; and you have persevered and have patience, and have labored for My name's sake and have not become weary.

Nevertheless I have this against you, that you have left your first love. Remember therefore from where you have fallen; repent and do the first works, or else I will come to you quickly and remove your lampstand from its place—unless you repent. But this you have, that you hate the deeds of the Nicolaitans, which I also hate.

He who has an ear, let him hear what the Spirit says to the churches. To him who overcomes I will give to eat from the tree of life, which is in the midst of the Paradise of God.

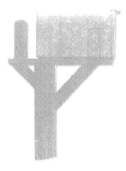

Chapter One - First Love

As a little kid, my first loves were Mexican food and baseball. My idea of heaven on earth was when we had a game on Tuesday because the post-game meal was always ten tacos for a dollar at Taco Tia, where my dad would buy a few bags full and bring it home to re-hash the game. Yum!

Then, from the third through the sixth grade, my love interest took human form in the person of a brown haired girl named Jenny. Of course, she never knew it. I was too shy and she was too perfect. Even though I had five sisters by this time, I was still paralyzed around Jenny. Finally, I believed by fate, our sixth grade teacher arranged the seating chart in a way that put me in the seat directly behind Jenny. Jackpot. A match made in heaven. I heard the Hallelujah Chorus and chapel bells. I visualized the moment that I would kneel between the desks and pledge my heart. Of course, as an introverted kid I didn't follow through on any of my plans, never even spoke to her, that I recall, and she probably never even knew I was back there. The next year we moved to a different state. But I never forgot *my first love*.

I caught a glimpse of true love a few years later when Mary Ann walked into my life. The first time I saw her I was smitten. The world stopped turning when she walked by. Her flowing auburn hair seemed to collect all the available sunlight and then release it back into the atmosphere with a warm, soft glow. She defined perfection. But it was her smile that captured my heart. For when her lips parted and her nose crinkled and she lit up the world with a big grin, a mouth full of glistening, silvery braces would shine forth in all their polished splendor. I tingle just thinking about it. I loved girls with braces! About six years later we were married, sometime along the way the braces came off, but by then I was in for life. *First love.*

Jesus has something to say to us about our first love. But He wants us to know a few things before we get to that, things that will give us hope and assurance that what He writes is for our good, things that remind us how well He really does know each of us.

He holds you and walks in your midst

To the angel of the church of Ephesus write, These things says He who holds the seven stars in His right hand, who walks in the midst of the seven golden lampstands.

In each letter, Jesus opens with a description of Himself that establishes a context for what He is about to say. In this case, the picture is of Christ holding seven stars and walking in the midst of seven lampstands. The apostle John, to whom Jesus is entrusting the letter, had previously received a vision of Christ which He describes in chapter one. In Revelation 1:20, Jesus explained the image of stars and lampstands that He uses again here. He said that the seven stars are the angels, or ministers, of the churches, and the lampstands are the churches themselves. Commentator Matthew Henry writes: *"(Ministers of Christ) are instruments in his hand, and all the good they do is done by his hand with them."*

What a beautiful picture of the present reality of Christ and His church. He holds His servants as stars in His hand and walks in their midst. Christ's living presence is an active reality.

Always a remnant

Ephesus was a major city in the region and, like most prominent cities, it attracted nuts and kooks of every stripe. It was the headquarters for a particular non-christian religious sect which wielded great economic and cultural influence (Acts 19:21-41), yet the community had one of the strongest Christian movements in the region. Isn't that an interesting dichotomy? Headquarters for an international cult which had its tentacles in everything from government to commerce, yet home to a thriving Christian presence.

The city of Ephesus is an example of one of the amazing truths of the Christian faith, which is how God consistently infiltrates evil strongholds with a remnant of believers who are able to stand firm in the face of opposition. Armed only with the love of God and the word of His grace they faithfully spread the message of hope in the midst of oppressive despair. We see it happening in our generation in Asia, Africa and the

Middle East in dramatic fashion among evil, militant regimes. Everywhere the enemy gains some level of momentum, the resilient church will be right along to shine the light of hope in the midst of despair and gloom. This was the case in Ephesus and is probably true of your town, where God has planted you and other followers of Christ, armed with that same love, equipped with the same message - that God loves people and He wants to make them whole and well through faith in Jesus Christ. In the same way He planted Paul in Ephesus, He has planted you and your church in a community where He holds you in His hand, and He walks in your midst, a remnant advancing the kingdom of heaven.

Walking in the midst of His church as a shepherd watchfully tending his flock, Christ is aware and acquainted with every word and every deed. Nothing slips by Him, nothing happens that He doesn't see. In the Ephesian church, He notes several things they were doing mostly right.

I know your works, your labor, your patience...

The Ephesian Christians were committed workers. They weren't just sitting on their hands, waiting for something spiritual to happen. They were about the Master's business, doers of the word and not hearers only. Being a hard worker is a good thing, and Jesus blesses them for their labor.

...and that you cannot bear those who are evil. And you have tested those who say they are apostles and are not, and have found them liars;

Their faith was well defined and well defended. They didn't run after every fad and fancy that came down the road. By this time in the first century, the church was several decades old, and there were plenty of people running around with new doctrines and teachings meant to improve and refine the message of Jesus, making it more contemporary and relevant to the changing world, with the convenient side effect of gathering followers for themselves. Paul had warned the Ephesian church leaders that this would happen and prepared them well. He said:

For I know this, that after my departure savage wolves will come in among you, not sparing the flock. Also from among yourselves men will rise up, speaking perverse things, to draw away the disciples after themselves. Therefore watch, and remember that for three years I did not cease to warn everyone night and day with tears. Acts 20:29-31

Paul warned this very church of people rising up, from within their midst, looking to draw away the disciples after themselves. The apostle took this inward threat very seriously. It broke his heart to think that fellow believers would divide God's church - but he also knew people, and he knew they would come.

Unfortunately, the problem of people following the latest theological twist has not lost its allure in the contemporary church. There is always someone rising up and stepping out to do it better or different or, in their minds at least, *correctly* - drawing people to themselves as they attempt to craft a truly successful (which usually means well attended) church. Many times, these selfish attempts at leading the church result in the commandments of Christ and the cost of discipleship being thrown out with the baptismal water and replaced with Five Steps to Marital Something, How to Be A Successful Whatever, or Seven Habits of This or That.

Paul warned the Ephesians to watch out, and watch out they did. They knew what they believed and why. Paul poured his heart out among them every day for around three years.

Could the same be said of you and your church? Are you mining the depths of God's word with an open heart and mind, or are you listening to three points and a conclusion from a great public speaker who rarely opens his Bible? It's important stuff. For this commendation to apply to us, it's got to be true in practice, not just theory. We have got to be discerning, clear thinking, spirit-filled, students of the word who can smell a wolf from across the street.

...and you have persevered and have patience, and have labored for My name's sake and have not become weary.

The Ephesian believers weren't quitters! They were tenacious, stalwart believers. One of the dynamics at work at this point in the first century, because of the fact that the Romans were tired of Christianity's influence and weary of their refusal to honor the emperor as God, was that persecution against Christians had begun in earnest. Emperors with a thirst for power and addiction to acclaim began terrorizing the Christians to the point of death.

Set against the physical persecution were the promises of Christ's return

"I will go and prepare a place for you, and if I go I will come again and receive you to Myself; that where I am, there you may be also." (See John 14:1-3).

In the world they were being persecuted, and in their meetings they would remind each other of the imminence of Christ's return. How they must have longed to hear the trumpet call of God as they awaited His second coming. The Ephesians were learning patience, expectantly looking forward to His return even though the pressure of life in the empire was difficult and persecution was intense. Jesus commends them for their ability to persevere under difficult circumstances.

Hard working, wise, and strong - all positive attributes that we would like to be said of ourselves. But really, aren't these things that could be said about any person under the right circumstances? There is nothing particularly christian or godly about these virtues. We all know people who are not yet christian who work harder than their co-workers. We know others who are wise and tactful, but, for some reason, are not yet christian. And the same goes for tenacity - soldiers, athletes, firefighters, to name a few, are people known for strength and perseverance. So while these attributes are positive, they seem to fall short of God's best. It is like Jesus is saying, "I'm glad this is true of you, but anyone can do this. I've got bigger things in mind for you. We've done larger and more significant things together in the past, and I'm writing this to help you remember that, to help you find the missing piece and get back to the real work of your calling."

While there may be positive, commendable things going on in my life, am I willing to consider that there may be a critical piece (or pieces) missing that would re-animate all that is stale and stagnant?

The missing piece

Nevertheless I have this against you, that you have left your first love.

The Ephesian Christians were hard workers, discerning, sound and persevering - all good things. But something was missing, something that negated the power and blessing from an otherwise strong church. They had left their first love.

I was still in my teens when I first read this letter, still trying to figure out the meaning of life, and still very new to the faith. At first I thought God was speaking to me about my third through sixth grade crush, Jenny, and I thought, "Oh no, I blew it and Jesus is holding it against me! I left my first love, I'm doomed!" I took this very seriously, as we all should. Then I realized - "Wait a minute, Mary Ann was my first *true* love, the first one where we were both actually involved, and I never left her, so maybe I could get by on a technicality."

I slowly began to understand that Jesus wasn't speaking about my physical love life as much as my *life's love*. Not my first relationship, but the relationship that was first.

The love that should be in foremost in all churches, and all Christians, is Jesus Christ. The love that the Ephesians had left or replaced with something else was their love for Christ Jesus himself. The New Testament describes love as the key to the relationship between God and mankind.

For God so loved the world that He gave His only begotten Son, that whoever believes in Him should not perish but have everlasting life. John 3:16

He who has My commandments and keeps them, it is he who loves Me. And he who loves Me will be loved by My Father, and I will love him and manifest Myself to him. John 14:21

Jesus answered and said to him, "If anyone loves Me, he will keep My word; and My Father will love him, and We will come to him and make Our home with him." John 14:23

Love is the core essence of relationship with God and the supreme evidence of a changed and redeemed life. The love of God at the heart of our lives and spiritual communities is the single most important attribute of kingdom life. Everything else, even our most commendable qualities and accomplishments, are nothing. Paul put it this way:

Though I speak with the tongues of men and of angels, but have not love, I have become sounding brass or a clanging cymbal. And though I have the gift of prophecy, and understand all mysteries and all knowledge, and though I have all faith, so that I could remove mountains, but have not love, I am nothing. And though I bestow all my goods to feed the poor, and though I give my body to be burned, but have not love, it profits me nothing. 1 Corinthians 13:1-3

Without love "I am nothing," and "I profit nothing." Pretty clear. Love is mandatory, love for Jesus is paramount. It's number one.

Love is also hard to quantify. How can I determine if I love God more than I love my dog, or more than my spouse or my Harley? We can easily say we love the Lord and that His love is paramount, but how do we know, how do we judge ourselves?

Do a self-check

When my car is making a funny noise, there are some basic things I can check myself before taking it to a mechanic. I can check the oil. A car with no oil will make a funny noise, at least for a while, until it stops running completely (voice of experience). I can check the radiator for water, check the tire inflation, check the belts and hoses. If we take some time to check the basics maybe we'll save ourselves the expense of a complete overhaul. It's kind of the same way with our love for God. There are some basic things we can check and take steps to correct. Here are a few:

1 - Check the joy in my Christian walk.

Have the things of God become commonplace? You've heard it all before, blah, blah, blah. Bible reading and prayer have lost their centrality in your life and you rarely open the bible, you rarely pray save the times you're called on. Christianity is your heritage, but not really a part of your day to day life. You find yourself responding more to the pastor's emotional illustrations than you do the meaning of the text. Still going through all the right motions, but not sure why any more, and you aren't even sure it's all necessary or worth it.

2 - Check your love for others.

As we walk with Jesus, learning to know Him, understanding His ways, experiencing His love, our love for Him should do more than plateau. It should increase more and more. The way loving God manifests itself in our lives is by loving people. We love Him, and it is expressed by our love for people. One of the key ways to check our love for God is to check our love for people. Because people can be pretty unlovable.

As we get older, it is common to gravitate to a few people with whom we are comfortable and avoid the rest. I've said myself, during weaker moments, "I love people, I just don't like them very much," which is a veiled way of saying I don't love people very much, a symptom of leaving my first love - because loving God shows up in our lives through loving people.

3 - Check your selfishness.

This one is tough because our culture drills happiness and fulfillment into each of us from such a young age. Being self-focused, striving to achieve and attain is drilled into each of us. It's equated with happiness and joy. Our teachers tell us that if we work hard now we will enjoy life later. It's all self-based. The confusing part is that following Christ accomplishes much the same thing in that we become truly happy and fulfilled in life.

The difference is that happiness and fulfillment for the culture is self-based and happiness and fulfillment in Christ are based on selflessness, giving freely as freely we have received. As Christians, we can be lured in, or back in, to the mentality that God wants the same things for us that we want, power, wealth, prestige, and we become selfish Christians. Much different from the selflessness Christ modeled:

For even the Son of Man did not come to be served, but to serve, and to give His life a ransom for many. Mark 10:45

Selflessness, preferring others over ourselves, should be a hallmark of the believer. When selfishness replaces selflessness and our personal comfort and satisfaction become our primary goals, what we think is love for Christ may actually be love of our self, which the Bible tells us will be a huge problem in the last days.

But know this, that in the last days perilous times will come: For men will be lovers of themselves, lovers of money, boasters, proud, blasphemers, disobedient to parents, unthankful, unholy, unloving, unforgiving, slanderers, without self-control, brutal, despisers of good, traitors, headstrong, haughty, lovers of pleasure rather than lovers of God, having a form of godliness but denying its power. And from such people turn away! 2 Tim. 3:1-5

Lovers of themselves, lovers of pleasure rather than lovers of God. Selfishness.

Abandoning our first love is such a significant, spiritual life or death issue, that Jesus sends the letter, preserves it over the centuries and sets it before each generation when the things of the world begin crowding out the purity and simplicity of our love for Jesus.

Remember, Repent and Repeat

Remember therefore from where you have fallen; repent and do the first works, or else I will come to you quickly and remove your lampstand from its place—unless you repent.

Remember. Repent. Repeat. Simple to say, hard to live. Can you remember how life changed when you first came to Christ? Can you remember your priorities, what you thought about, the way you spent your time and how you used your money and talents? For those of us who came to Jesus a little later in life, we remember that our world turned upside down. We had a hunger and thirst for the things of God; we found His Spirit changing our attitudes and actions; we began accepting and loving people for whom we had no time before. It was a revolution of heart, soul, mind and strength - and the best thing that ever happened to us, the single best decision we ever made. And we found ourselves loving Him more as the days went by.

For others, you were brought up knowing God's love - from Bible stories at bedtime to mother's heartfelt prayers, from dressing up for church to attending daily Vacation Bible School. You may have asked Jesus into your heart at four or five or eight years of age, and you honestly can't remember a time when you didn't know His love. "How can I leave something I've always known?" you might ask yourself, and it's a good question. But think about it this way. Back in those childhood days of faith, how would you describe your love for God? How about consummate, unqualified, without limit and unconditional? Your love for God was childlike and pure; it was as real as anything in life; it helped you go to sleep at night and face monsters under the bed. He was with you and, like the little boy named David, you were invincible at His side. Would that still be a fitting description today? Maybe. But the world tries its best to force childlike faith to be squeezed and tempered and left behind. And that is unfortunate.

So Jesus says to repent. That means to change direction, change your mind, change your course, turn around. Repentance isn't casual, it is an acknowledgment of my own shortcomings and Christ's sufficiency, the adequacy of His finished work on the cross to cover me and cloth me in His righteousness. It is reckoning myself dead, crucified with Christ, and enlivened by His power. I turn from my sin and cry out for a clean heart.

Have mercy upon me, O God, According to Your lovingkindness; according to the multitude of Your tender mercies, blot out my transgressions. Wash me thoroughly from my iniquity, and cleanse me from my sin... Create in me a clean heart, O God, and renew a steadfast spirit within me. Psalm 51:1-2, 10

Remember, repent and repeat. Repeat those things you did in the early days of faith. Live simply, love deeply, get your faith off the shelf and out of your head and get it back into your hands and feet. Live with that confidence and assurance in Christ that once marked your prayers and your actions.

Serious consequences

It is a critical admonition. Jesus is not making a suggestion here; He is giving a directive that will have consequences if ignored. He says that, if we do not repent, "(He) will come to you quickly and remove your lampstand from its place..." Now, since the lampstand represents the church, it's easy to picture Jesus reaching out and taking hold of our grand building with its steeple and columns and pews and picking it up and removing it from its place, kind of like King Kong ripping his way through town, uprooting buildings and tossing them out of his path. But remember, Jesus doesn't think of a building when He talks about His church. When Jesus thinks of His church, He thinks of people, the precious children for whom He died. So what "place" do God's people hold, from which they could be removed by Christ if they do not repent?

His church does hold a place in society. It is a place that only His church can hold. It's the ministry of redemption, the role of sharing the good news of the gospel with the world through the power of the Holy Spirit. I think Jesus says He will remove the lampstand He is speaking of the power of the Holy Spirit working through His body. It might be that what was once a vital movement, led by the Spirit, flowing in power, bringing the good news of the gospel to the nations, slowly leaves their first love, most likely without even realizing it. Maybe they begin to let immorality have a secret place in the ministry and they begin subconsciously hide from the living God. Or their nemesis could be their very success as they create a brilliant business plan and begin to achieve results outside of the power of the Spirit and the hard work of intercession and dirty work of loving people, and they stop consciously depending on Christ.

So Jesus comes to visit one day and He looks around, like He did in the temple on the day of His triumphal entry, and He doesn't say anything, He just observes, watches to see if anybody notices the King. He watches the money-changers and the activity and the show. And He sees that they have left Him for another love. He leaves and He takes the lampstand with Him.

There is sure to be a spiritual community, a people who are willing to put Him on the throne, to surrender to Him and keep Him in first place in their hearts and actions. He'll do the work of redemption through them instead. Their lampstand will be the people among whom the fire of God shines and burns. And those, who were once at the heart of God's work in the world, are removed from use. Their lampstand is removed from its place.

They remain open for business, but Jesus is long gone.

I think this is the sad story of the church from about the fourth century on. It seems like whenever a movement was ignited by the flame of God's fire and began to turn the world upside down with God's love and power, they would go on for awhile, a decade or two, maybe even a hundred years. But eventually, in an attempt to retain their strong position, they set up rigid distinctive's that became more important, in practice, than a living relationship with Christ, and they leave their first love, and they die - Jesus leaves. They are no longer the heart of His work because He is no longer at the heart of theirs.

Jesus, then everybody else

But this you have, that you hate the deeds of the Nicolaitans, which I also hate.

The word Nicolaitan comes from two Greek words that suggest authority, (nicao) and people (laos), which has given some commentators the idea that the deeds of the Nicolaitans included the establishment of a hierarchy in the church separating clergy from laity. It's hard to be certain exactly what Jesus was referring to here, but certainly the idea of separating clergy and laity was something that He warned against:

But you, do not be called 'Rabbi'; for One is your Teacher, the Christ, and you are all brethren. Matthew 23:8

The hierarchy, or management structure, of the church of Christ is pretty simple. There is Jesus, the Teacher and Christ, the "head" of the body, and then there is the body under the head, that's all the rest of us, the church. No one is higher or closer or better, we are all simply followers, workers, believers, Christians, brothers and sisters in Christ. Isn't that a relief? Whether you stand behind a pulpit and preach or sit in a porch swing and pray. You are both the same, different gifts, talents and ministries, but the same Spirit working in us and through us. That is the simple structure of the Body of Christ - Jesus is the head, and the rest of us make up the body.

Just one head, and it's not you.

For there is one God and one Mediator between God and men, the Man Christ Jesus, I Timothy 2:5

Any structure or authority system which places people, even really good people, in between Christ and His church, is a bad idea, and Jesus hates it.

How about the modern church, do we hate what Jesus hated, or do we embrace it? We certainly preach the "priesthood of all believers" and equality in the body where

"There is neither Jew nor Greek, there is neither slave nor free, there is neither male nor female; for you are all one in Christ Jesus." (Galatians 3:28.)

But in practice, we do seem to separate people on the basis of their gifts. We have professional clergy, whole stables of specialized professional ministers with streamlined organizational structures and flowcharts. And no matter the denomination or tradition, we all do basically the same thing in our weekend services, whether trendy and contemporary or quiet and traditional. We sit listening mainly to the pros. And maybe, without intending to, we are suggesting to each other and to the world that there is a separation of rank in the church. Jesus is on top, no question in our minds about that. But under Jesus we've created a professional class, the leaders, those who tell the rest of us what to do, how to live, grow and serve. Last but not least there are the followers, the flock, the congregation.

Some might argue that their church tradition doesn't separate clergy from laity. "Oh, we don't have clergy, we have pastors that lead like shepherds." "We have a minister that dutifully serves," "Ours is a life coach, not some archaic priest." Maybe so, but I still wonder if Jesus sees any leftover Nicolaitanism lurking in the church today. If He does, and you can trust me on this, He still doesn't like it.

He who has an ear, let him hear what the Spirit says to the churches. To him who overcomes I will give to eat from the tree of life, which is in the midst of the Paradise of God.

If you have ears, listen to what the Holy Spirit is saying through this letter. But, even if you don't have ears or are as deaf as a stone, you are not off the hook, because the listening He is speaking of isn't with our physical ears, but with our spiritual senses, our recognition and understanding of His voice.

When we tell you these things, we do not use words that come from human wisdom. Instead, we speak words given to us by the Spirit, using the Spirit's words to explain spiritual truths. But people who aren't spiritual can't receive these truths from God's Spirit. It all sounds foolish to them and they can't understand it, for only those who are spiritual can understand what the Spirit means. 1 Corinthians 2:13-14 NLT

So, you need to be spiritual to understand what the Spirit is saying. You need to be a christian, a spirit-filled follower of Christ to really understand the message Jesus is communicating. Those outside of Christ may be engaged or enraged by reading His word, but, until it kindles faith in their heart to know Him, it will just be ink on a page.

But to those with ears, those who are serious, although sometimes misguided, followers of Christ, He adds with hope, confidence and faith, "to him who overcomes," that is, if you have left your first love, or have slipped into any of the other ruts that Jesus mentions, He has every hope and expectation that you will respond and overcome, and He offers the wonderful promise of fruit from the tree of life.

In Revelation 22, we read that people in heaven will enjoy the fruit of the tree of life, a different fruit in every season. What a wonderful promise and treat that is awaiting the overcomers. There is a Tree of Life available to overcomers in this life, as well, through a relationship with Jesus Christ. When we repent and place Jesus in the central place of honor and love in our heart, *He* will be our strength and energy for life. Like food for the body, nourishing us abundantly with His love, joy and peace,

covering us with grace, acceptance and forgiveness,
different fruit for every season and circumstance of life.

To the angel of the church in Smyrna write,

These things says the First and the Last, who was dead, and came to life: "I know your works, tribulation, and poverty (but you are rich); and I know the blasphemy of those who say they are Jews and are not, but are a synagogue of Satan.

Do not fear any of those things which you are about to suffer. Indeed, the devil is about to throw some of you into prison, that you may be tested, and you will have tribulation ten days. Be faithful until death, and I will give you the crown of life.

He who has an ear, let him hear what the Spirit says to the churches. He who overcomes shall not be hurt by the second death.

Chapter Two - You Can Make It

Have you ever noticed how a name can describe something about the person or place? Take my name for instance, Ed. Why is it that the goofy, dimwitted sidekick is always named Ed in the movies? Or "Earl,"same thing. It seems like the loser cousin or the redneck, crooked toothed friend with the 1979 Pinto, is always either Ed or Earl. Never the hero, never the star. Ed-Earl is always going to get hit by a bus or have his pants set on fire at some point in the show. That stereotype drives me crazy because my name happens to be Edward Earl.

In the Bible, names often relate to some eventual personality trait or characteristic of the person. Take twin brothers Jacob and Esau, sons of Isaac and Rebekah, and grandsons of Abraham. You almost always hear Jacob named first, but he was actually born second. Big brother Esau was named "Hairy" because he was a furry little guy. His brother was born moments later, hanging on to Harry's foot, so they named him Jacob, or heel-grabber. More specifically, Jacob means supplanter, which is taking the place of another through force, scheming or strategy.

He was grabbing at the hairy little foot in front of him as if trying to squeeze past him and take his brother's place in the birth order. Ultimately, Jacob became a supplanter in life when he dressed up like his brother and deceived his father into giving him the blessing of the firstborn son, effectively taking the place of his brother, not by force like he tried at birth, but by scheming. Names matter.

One of the things that makes the letter to Smyrna particularly interesting is how the circumstances of the church relate so specifically to the name of the community. The name Smyrna contains the root word "myrrh" which was a substance used in biblical times for its fragrance. Myrrh was the sap from particular trees that hardened and could be packaged and sold. To use the myrrh, you would break it, crush it, or burn it, thus causing the fragrant oils to emit the bittersweet aroma. It had various applications, but the key idea is that the fragrance was activated as the resin was crushed.

As myrrh suffers, fragrance is released.

The Christian people in Smyrna understood suffering. They knew what it felt like to be persecuted and crushed. But, in keeping with their name, their affliction released a sweet, spiritual aroma, the fragrance of Christ, filling the church and the city with a sense of His love and forgiveness.

Now thanks be to God who always leads us in triumph in Christ, and through us diffuses the fragrance of His knowledge in every place. For we are to God the fragrance of Christ among those who are being saved and among those who are perishing. To the one we are the aroma of death leading to death, and to the other the aroma of life leading to life. 2 Corinthians 2:14-16

The believers in Smyrna filled the city with the fragrance of His knowledge through brokenness and suffering. The same will be true of you in a season of persecution or affliction - you will diffuse the fragrance of Christ in the place you live and among the people you serve. Suffering activates the fragrance of Christ.

Unwitting human agents of evil

Satan uses two basic methods of assault against the christian witness in the world, persecution and infiltration. Either head-on persecution, seeking to make Christians give up or shut down, or by infiltrating the ranks, like weeds growing among the wheat, introducing sin into the camp of the godly. He'll use one method or the other, both if necessary. And the primary way He carries out the campaign is through people. Even as God uses people to accomplish His righteous purpose in the world by the power of the Holy Spirit, Satan uses unwitting humans as agents in his evil campaign against the church and against humanity.

By example, back in the first century, around the time Jesus was dictating this letter to John, there lived a certain man from a severely dysfunctional home. At age three, his father, a murdering cheat, died. His mother married again but eventually poisoned the boy's stepfather by feeding him a dish of tainted mushrooms. The young man committed his first murder soon afterward by slaying a teenager who opposed him. He killed his first two wives and, in order to marry a third time, he murdered the husband of the woman he sought. In time, he also arranged for the murder of his mother. Through all this, the scoundrel was able to rise to popular acclaim; but, by age thirty-one, his evil deeds had caught up with him, and he was sentenced to death. Before he could be executed, he slit his own throat. The name of this bottom-dwelling thug was Nero. Caesar Nero was the emperor of Rome for about fourteen years in the middle of the first century. This is the same Nero who lit the evil fire of persecution upon the church that led to a kind of genocide wherein countless numbers of Christians were martyred during Roman dominance.

Nero was a willing accomplice of the evil one. Satan looks for people like this, people with a lust for power and a thirst for blood. There has always been this element of evil, physical persecution, active against the church of Jesus Christ in some region of the world.

Things were bad in Roman times - the cruelty unbelievable. But, in the 20th century more believers were killed for their faith than in all the other centuries combined. Even today, many brothers and sisters are being separated from families, imprisoned, tortured and executed for their faith in Jesus Christ. Under radical regimes around the world Christians have become the scapegoats of choice as they are singled out for campaigns of hate and terror. It is to the people of suffering in the world that Jesus writes.

Jesus conquered death

These things says the First and the Last, who was dead, and came to life:

Jesus begins by pointing us back to His resurrection. The Christians of Smyrna were only a generation removed from the resurrection of Christ, the cornerstone of the faith, well aware of the revolution that it caused in the world. The resurrection forever changed the playing field of life and death, because, when Christ rose from the dead, death was defeated. It lost its power over the world, lost the finality of its sting. Jesus said:

Jesus said unto her, I am the resurrection, and the life: he that believeth in me, though he were dead, yet shall he live. John 11:25 KJV

A little while longer and the world will see Me no more, but you will see Me. Because I live, you will live also. John 14:19

Now if you are young and strong and living in a peaceable society, that may not seem like such dramatic news. But if you know the frailty of life, the pain of suffering for your faith or the heartbreak of losing someone you love, it is the best news of all time! Jesus Christ conquered death. He led the way. Death no longer marks the bitter end. Christ's resurrection changed the last chapter of our book, death is not the end. Jesus, the first and the last, the beginning and the end, has gone before humanity and removed deaths finality. Eternal life is awaiting each believer because of Christ.

Many Christians in Smyrna, including their pastor, Polycarp, had been killed for their faith, by sword and by fire, and these words would be etched forever in the hearts of loved ones silently watching from the shadows, "though he were dead, yet shall he live."

Jesus knows

I know your works, and tribulation, and poverty, But you are rich).

"I know." Don't skip over those first two words as you race to the "you are rich" part. All the circumstances and situations and troubling people that you've dealt with, which others can never fully comprehend, Jesus knows about. He says, "I know your works." The word there for works suggests distress or pressure. Jesus is saying, "I know the pressure you are under, I hear your distress, I see your tribulation." These people were in bad shape; they were going through a hellish existence because of their allegiance to Christ. How it must have grieved Jesus to watch them, feeling their pain as He recalled facing the same opposition, and worse, in His life. It must have been all He could do to keep from sending a legion of angels to destroy their oppressors. And it has been the same way throughout time, as He observes the injustice foisted upon believers due to their love for God and freedom in Christ.

But, He also knows something that is not physically evident. And that is the glorious inheritance we have in Him. Having been adopted by God, we have become joint heirs with Christ, and the glory of the kingdom of heaven is eternally ours. We are rich in ways that defy description and understanding. And, while it is hard to bask in that hope during seasons of tribulation, it remains true, regardless of the outward appearance or circumstances of our earthly life. We are rich in Christ.

And I know the blasphemy of them which say they are Jews, and are not, but are the synagogue of Satan.

Much of the trouble in the life of Christ and in the early church was instigated by the leaders of the Jewish synagogues. They claimed to follow God but, in truth, were not worshippers of God at all. They had rituals steeped in tradition and their coveted lineage, but in Jesus' eyes, they were the synagogues of Satan, not synagogues of God. In John, chapter eight, Jesus and some of the Jewish leaders have this exchange:

They answered and said to Him, "Abraham is our father."

Jesus said to them, "If you were Abraham's children, you would do the works of Abraham... You are of your father the devil, and the desires of your father you want to do... John 8:39,44a

The blasphemy, or irreverent behavior, of these false Jews was their slander of the Messiah, claiming to follow God but ignoring His promised Deliverer, Jesus Christ. With lying and twisted words, these Jews sought to turn popular consensus against Jesus and anyone who would follow Him. They accused the Christians of being cannibals because they received communion and spoke of the body and blood of Christ; they proclaimed that the Christians were atheists because they did not attend synagogue or at least a pagan temple; the Christians spoke of being a body, and members one of another, so they were accused of sexual perversion.

Lies, slander, ridicule. Not so different from the position taken against Christians by some in our day. Believers, in the eyes of some vocal critics, are a bunch of right-winged, fundamentalist lunatics that seek only to take away all the rights of women, impose puritan morality and turn the clock back 100 years. And, if they say it loud enough and long enough, it becomes part of the public conscience even though it couldn't be further from the truth. Jesus reminds us that Satan is behind it all, using unwitting human agents to accomplish his devilish scheme of silencing the message of Christ in the world.

There is a limit

Do not fear any of those things which you are about to suffer. Indeed, the devil is about to throw some of you into prison, that you may be tested, and you will

have tribulation ten days. Be faithful until death, and I will give you the crown of life.

Jesus knows what they have been through, He knows the pressure they are currently under and He says, basically, "It's going to get worse before it gets better." See it there, "Do not fear any of those things which you are about to suffer." Wow! The Christians in Smyrna have been under the torturous hand of persecution for some time, and, instead of finding solace, they are told that it is going to get worse.

Have you ever been to the end of your rope? Taken all the sickness, rebellion, heartache and tribulation you can bear? How encouraging would it be to be told, "Friend, don't be afraid, but it's going to get worse." To hear something like that would surely knock the wind out of you and you might rightly think, "I don't know if I can take much more of this."

But, before we drop our hands and give up, Jesus provides a curious detail that brings new perspective to the upcoming season of trial.

It's going to last ten days.

Scholars don't really know what Jesus meant by ten days of tribulation. Some have suggested that it refers to the ten periods of Roman persecution, while others say it refers to ten literal days of prolonged attack. But whatever "ten days" refers to, it means that Jesus is determining the limits, not Satan. The period of suffering cannot go beyond the limits Jesus has set. There is no power in hell or on earth that could extend this trial to eleven days. It won't go eleven. It won't go twelve. Christ Jesus sets a boundary beyond which Satan cannot go.

Whatever it is you are going through, whatever suffering and trial you are being afflicted with by the enemy of your soul, there is a limit, and Jesus has already determined it! Whether you are in day one or day eight, the good news is that Jesus has defined the limits to the distress and tribulation over your life. He knows you better than you know yourself and He knows that you can make it. If you couldn't, He wouldn't let it continue. Take a moment and say this out loud a few times, letting it sink into your heart and soul;

"I can make it ten days. Jesus defines the limits of my suffering, not Satan. I will make it. I can do all things through Christ who gives strengthens me. With Christ's strength, I will make it ten days!"

Then Jesus adds, "be faithful unto death." Now does that mean that they would be dying for their faith? Yes, some would. Many did, and more Christians around the world will, even this week. But it also means that however long life is, through everything that comes your way, remain faithful. Be faithful unto death. Remain faithful if you live another fifty years; remain faithful through thick and thin; remain faithful unto death whether it comes tomorrow through persecution, or thirty years from now due to old age, and you will receive a crown of life.

A curious crown

What a great crown! This isn't a crown of gold; it's not a crown of jewels, this crown is made of a different material altogether. The crown being fitted for the faithful is made of life. Can you imagine a crown of life? I don't know what it looks like but I know there are many people, some of our own loved ones, who are wearing theirs even now. And I know that Jesus has one ready for each of His precious, faithful, persevering children.

Paul describes this reward a little differently when, with the dramatic imagery of heaven, he writes:

For we know that if our earthly house, this tent, is destroyed, we have a building from God, a house not made with hands, eternal in the heavens. For in this we groan, earnestly desiring to be clothed with our habitation which is from heaven, if indeed, having been clothed, we shall not be found naked. For we who are in this tent groan, being burdened, not because we want to be unclothed, but further clothed, that mortality may be swallowed up by life. 2 Corinthians 5:1-4

What a stirring image of the victorious Christian, having faithfully passed through the fiery trial of Satan's fury, our bodies literally groaning for the safe harbor of our heavenly home. Then to arrive, having mortality swallowed up, but not by death, for death has lost its sting, death has been stripped of its power over you - mortality will be swallowed up, by life! That is the crown that awaits the faithful.

He who has an ear, let him hear what the Spirit says to the churches. He who overcomes shall not be hurt by the second death.

Overcomers will not be hurt by the second death. The second death is described in Revelation chapter twenty, when all humanity, excluding Christ's followers, will stand before the Great White Throne Judgment of God. Death and hell will give up their dead, and all who are not written in the Lamb's Book of Life shall be cast into Gehenna, the second death. If the Great White Throne Judgement leads to the second death, what is the first?

There are two deaths. Every person must, eventually, die physically. No one lives forever in the flesh and blood body, we all grow old, decay and die. So go long before their time and some live for a hundred years or more but everyone, eventually, will die. That's the first death.

The second death can happen two ways: For many, the second death comes when we trust Christ and "die" to sin. In a very real sense, by faith we are crucified with Christ, nevertheless we live. This death is pictured at our water baptism when we are "buried" in the water as Christ was buried in the tomb and we rise to a new life in Christ, even as He conquered death and rose from the grave. In this sense, we experience the second death before the first death, we die to sin through faith in Christ before we actually die physically.

For the person who rejects Christ, after dying physically after this life (the first death), the second death represents the eternal separation from God that will be handed down from the Great White Throne.

Our eternal destiny is decided in this life as the choice is made to receive Christ and be separated from sin now, dying to sin through faith in Jesus Christ. Or to reject Christ in this life and be separated from God for eternity at the final judgment. Die to sin now through faith in Christ and the second death will become a non-issue in your personal life.

And to the angel of the church in Pergamos write,

These things says He who has the sharp two-edged sword: "I know your works, and where you dwell, where Satan's throne is. And you hold fast to My name, and did not deny My faith even in the days in which Antipas was My faithful martyr, who was killed among you, where Satan dwells. But I have a few things against you, because you have there those who hold the doctrine of Balaam, who taught Balak to put a stumbling block before the children of Israel, to eat things sacrificed to idols, and to commit sexual immorality. Thus you also have those who hold the doctrine of the Nicolaitans, which thing I hate. Repent, or else I will come to you quickly and will fight against them with the sword of My mouth.

He who has an ear, let him hear what the Spirit says to the churches. To him who overcomes I will give some of the hidden manna to eat. And I will give him a white stone, and on the stone a new name written which no one knows except him who receives it.

Chapter Three - A Grey World

Satan is a chameleon who will do anything to destroy peoples lives. If he fails to derail the church from her Divine calling through a frontal attack of physical persecution as exampled by Smyrna, he will change tactics and try to get a foothold on the inside, becoming an angel of light, a wolf in sheep's clothing.

For such are false apostles, deceitful workers, transforming themselves into apostles of Christ. And no wonder! For Satan himself transforms himself into an angel of light. Therefore it is no great thing if his ministers also transform themselves into

ministers of righteousness, whose end will be according to their works. 2 Corinthians 11:13-15

In this strategy, the chameleon appears, not as a venomous serpent, but rather a harmless lamb or well meaning shepherd, slowly and methodically persuading a church to lower the sights of their mission, coddle up to prevailing cultural norms, and exchange black and white for grey. This is what was happening at Pergamos, Satan had infiltrated the ranks.

And to the angel of the church in Pergamos write, These things says He who has the sharp two-edged sword

Jesus introduces Himself with reference to the vision John saw in Revelation, chapter one:

"out of His mouth went a sharp two-edged sword." (1:16)

Jesus doesn't hold a sword in His hand, as a man would wield a weapon. Instead the sword extends from his mouth, and the sword is the Word of God. His Word is likened to a sword in the book of Hebrews:

For the word of God is living and powerful, and sharper than any two-edged sword, piercing even to the division of soul and spirit, and of joints and marrow, and is a discerner of the thoughts and intents of the heart. Hebrews 4:12

Jesus speaks the Word of God - definitive, absolute and true. Sharp enough to divide soul from spirit, joints from marrow. So sharp that it separates our words from actions and thoughts from intentions. Jesus with the two-edged sword reminds us that saying things we think God expects to hear will never cover a compromised heart. If Satan has successfully infiltrated a life, God's word will both reveal it and rebut any denial.

I know your works, and where you dwell, where Satan's throne is. And you hold fast to My name, and did not deny My faith even in the days in which Antipas was My faithful martyr, who was killed among you, where Satan dwells.

Jesus reminds the church that He knows their works. The fact that He mentions this every time suggests that it is something that He wants us to hear. Whether I am in a crowded room, or all alone in the basement, He sees me, knows what I am doing, and, just in case I think I'm in a shadow that is outside His view, He reminds me, seven times in seven letters, that this is not the case. He knows exactly what I am doing. While that should convict your socks off if you are engaged in activity that you shouldn't be. Don't think this is all bad, though, because if you have ever wondered if God sees those good things you do in secret, He does. He knows your works - all of them. There is no need to toot your own horn; in fact, resist the urge to tell people how great you are.

"your Father who sees in secret will reward you openly." Matthew 6:18.

He knows where you live

"I know your works, a*nd where you dwell...*" The apostle Paul highlighted this point in Acts when he said:

From one man he made every nation of men, that they should inhabit the whole earth; and he determined the times set for them and the exact places where they should live. Acts 17:26 NIV

How is that for specific? God has determined not only the time of our life, but also the exact places we should live. Even though I wish I had grown up in the fifties because I like the cars, God ordained when and where I would live, strategically placing me in His kingdom, like Queen Esther, for "such a time as this." (Esther 4:14)

Jesus knows what we are doing, knows where we live, and, for the people in Pergamos, Jesus knew something else that they probably didn't realize, Satan's throne was in their city. Not only his throne, but verse 13 tells us that Satan actually lived there. Keep in mind that Satan is a created being. He is a fallen angel; he is not omniscient like God. He can only be in one place at a time. When he was cast out of heaven, a number of the angels were cast out with him, and they are spread around the globe doing his bidding like ants at a picnic. But the fact remains that Satan, although a great angelic being, and the fallen angels we refer to as demons, can only be in one place at a time. And during the time Jesus dictated this letter, their devilish headquarters was somehow and in a realm we can see with our physical eyes, in Pergamos.

It's creepy to imagine that Satan's throne is somewhere on earth, but, as Jesus writes, it is. Even though God hasn't revealed where that command post is in our day, one thing is certain. Wherever Satan's throne is in these days, Christ is at work building a people of grace there. Satan might have lived in Pergamos, but Jesus still had a church there shining the light of truth in the darkness!

**... where sin abounded, grace abounded much more"
Romans 5:20.**

Jesus commended the church because they "held fast to
My name and did not deny the faith." The price for such
allegiance was high, persecution, torture, even death. Jesus
mentions Antipas, a brother in the church that had given
his life for his faith in Christ. Antipas means "against all,"
which is sometimes how it feels in the world as an
ambassador for Christ. Most of us have felt at times like
we might be the only one who is serious about Christ, the
only one willing to take a stand. Of course, that is never
the case. There are always other believers near, always a
remnant out sharing the Good News, doing the work of
the kingdom. And even if there weren't, Christ Himself is
always with you, always in you, and that fact alone is
enough to put ten thousand to flight should the need
arise.

To "hold fast the name of Jesus," is to declare the true
identity of Jesus Christ, His humanity and deity. Jesus was
fully man and fully God. This is the core the Christian
faith because other religions and cults cannot reconcile
these two. They say He was one or the other, a God who
wasn't really human, or a man who wasn't really God. But
Jesus was both. He was God incarnate, "in the flesh."

"Keeping the faith of Jesus," on the other hand, refers more to His life, how He came to earth and what He did while He was here: the virgin birth, His example of love, acceptance and forgiveness, His death on the cross, burial, and resurrection from the dead. Keeping the faith of Jesus is continuing to rely on and uphold the historical and spiritual truths of Jesus' life.

This is the ongoing charge to the body of Christ, to keep our focus on these two, primary truths - who He is and what He did. Keeping these doctrines at our core will help protect us from the encroachment of the enemy whether by persecution or cunning.

Regional stronghold

In every region of the world, Satan will assign demons to exploit the sinful choices of the people residing there in order to create an invisible fortress, or stronghold of sin, which grips society in ways the people don't even realize. These strongholds originate from selfish choices and are fortified by demonic forces in order to create an impregnable prison in which people are held spiritually captive. Here in Pergamos, as the seat of Satan's throne, the grip was great indeed. This community was in spiritual bondage because of their practices of idol worship, sexual immorality, and adherence to the Imperial cult, which espoused worshipping the Roman emperor as god. The society of Pergamos viewed these behaviors and belief systems as natural and normal conduct for life, unaware that these were the very tools Satan devised to hold the region in spiritual bondage to him.

Sneaking into the church

Now, while the church of Jesus Christ, the called out ones, would never willingly bow down to the emperor, commit sexual immorality as a normal way of life, or have anything to do with wooden idols, these culturally acceptable, non-Christian behaviors, were still able to sneak into the church. Satan just needed to make some spiritual-sounding adjustments, and the church took the bait hook, line and sinker. Jesus says it like this:

But I have a few things against you, because you have there those who hold the doctrine of Balaam, who taught Balak to put a stumbling block before the children of Israel, to eat things sacrificed to idols, and to commit sexual immorality. Thus you also have those who hold the doctrine of the Nicolaitans, which thing I hate.

The spiritual sounding way that Satan infiltrated and led the church to compromise was through the teaching of Balaam and the teaching of the Nicolaitans. Balaam, (Numbers 22-24, 31:16; 2 Peter 2:15; Jude 1:11) was a prophet of God, and an opportunist who misdirected the children of Israel for selfish gain through idol worship and fornication. Idol worship is putting anything, a carved symbol, a wooden pole, a new Mercedes, even your own selfish ambition, in front of God. If it takes your allegiance, time, resources and love, it's your idol. Sexual immorality has to do with putting myself before God. In sexual lust, we place our unquenchable thirst for fleshly satisfaction ahead of God. Idolatry and immorality are Balaam's doctrine.

The teaching of the Nicolaitans, which Jesus mentions in his letter to the Ephesians (2:1-7) as being "deeds," had blossomed in Pergamos into full-fledged doctrine. This is the idea of putting people before God or between God and mankind, as a go-between or hierarchy. Remember back in the old testament when the children of Israel wanted a king? They wanted to be like the other nations around them and have a leader, someone to follow, to make the rules. They already had a King. God was their King. He was the King of Kings and the Lord of Lords. But that wasn't good enough, that required faith. They wanted a person, someone they could see and applaud and follow around, someone to make decisions for them. Bring that idea into the first century church in a country that is already accustomed to bowing down to an emperor, and, after Jesus had ascended to heaven and the apostles had, for the most part, gone to be with the Lord, some people got the idea that there should be some kind of structure set up for the church, thus, the doctrine of the Nicolaitans - a spiritual pecking order with priests and holy people to mediate, to stand before God on your behalf, and then, to represent God to the people. And these people were set up on a pedestal, not unlike the place the emperor held in the culture at large.

And false teaching crept into the church, putting people, things and self in front of God; using religious sounding lingo, but in their essence, just watered down versions of the same strongholds with which Satan had shackled the prevailing culture. Instead of bowing prostrate before a wooden idol, it might have been setting up some Christian statue in memory of one of the apostles or someone; instead of participating in a sex orgy, maybe it was sexual fantasy or something of the like; instead of worshipping the emperor, it could have been undo spiritual dependency or adulation of a minister or priest. Same core problems, different wrapping.

This is why the church must remain vigilant, prayerful and committed to discipleship through the word of God. If we don't, this type of encroachment will inevitably happen. There will be weeds sown among the wheat, and the church will become no different from the world as we innocently and subtly conform to trends and customs of the world. We become compromised and ineffective.

As we consider our world today, please realize that whatever the overriding strongholds are in your region or city, Satan will take those very same things, wrap them up in Christian language, and use them to attempt infiltration in the church. You've got to be watchful, because the Lord won't stand for it.

Repent, or else I will come to you quickly and will fight against them with the sword of My mouth.

Notice Jesus says that He will come to "you" and fight against "them." Jesus comes to separate the weeds from the wheat, and He does it by His word. In the parable Jesus said that the weeds and the wheat would grow up together, and that's a prophetic truth, but one day, as He declares here, they will be separated by the Word of Truth. It is nothing for the discerner of the thoughts and intentions of the heart to root out and eradicate those infected by Satan. He could cleanse the body in an instant and without warning, but the letter here is so full of grace because Jesus is giving the church notice that judgement is imminent and it is time to correct our course. What a loving, compassionate God we serve.

He who has an ear, let him hear what the Spirit says to the churches. To him who overcomes I will give some of the hidden manna to eat. And I will give him a white stone, and on the stone a new name written which no one knows except him who receives it.

What a wonderful promise for those who shake free from the bondage of sin. First, a meal of hidden manna. This is a beautiful picture of the adequacy of Christ. Jesus Christ is enough, He is more than enough to supply our every need. Manna was "angel food" given directly by God to the children of Israel in the desert. Manna represents Jesus. He said He was the bread that came down from heaven, the bread of life, just like the manna that was send to the children of Israel.

Therefore they said to Him, "What sign will You perform then, that we may see it and believe You? What work will You do? Our fathers ate the manna in

the desert; as it is written, 'He gave them bread from heaven to eat.'"

Then Jesus said to them, "Most assuredly, I say to you, Moses did not give you the bread from heaven, but My Father gives you the true bread from heaven. For the bread of God is He who comes down from heaven and gives life to the world."

Then they said to Him, "Lord, give us this bread always."

And Jesus said to them, "I am the bread of life. He who comes to Me shall never hunger, and he who believes in Me shall never thirst. John 6:30-35

He who comes to Jesus shall never hunger, and he who believes in Him shall never thirst. There is no need to put something or someone in front of Jesus, He is adequate for every need.

After the manna is a white stone. He says that the overcomers shall receive a white stone, and the stone will have a new name written on it, that no one knows except the one receiving it. What a beautiful glimpse of the intimacy that exists between Jesus and each of His children. He gives you a personal name that is just between you and Him. Can you imagine what that must be like? A special, personal name given only to you from your heavenly Father?

We sometimes have special names for our wives and husbands, Honey, Sweetie, Sweetheart or some other. You don't call other people's spouses these names. If you did, you'd likely get a confused look or maybe a sock on the nose. Because they wouldn't understand the term coming from anyone other than their special person. Jesus is going to give you a special name like that, one just between you and Him.

This special, intimate name that is given to you is written on a white stone. I love this part. Some cultures used to vote by using black and white stones. You drop one or the other into the ballot box to cast your vote. A black stone was a No vote. You've heard of someone being "black-balled." That means they were rejected, or voted out. Whereas the white stone was a Yes vote, you are in. Accepted.

If you are like me, then you are no stranger to feelings of rejection. Our culture has that one honed to a fine edge, doesn't it. Rejection is commonplace in our society. But, over and against that, we have this promise from Jesus, that overcomers will receive a white stone from Him. A yes vote. Accepted. If Jesus votes Yes for you - you're in! His is the deciding vote. Doesn't that feel good? Knowing that Jesus has cast His vote for you?

Jesus is more than enough for your every need. He has an intimate name picked out, just for you. And a white stone, a "yes" vote that declares for all time and eternity that you are accepted. Amen!

And to the angel of the church in Thyatira write,

These things says the Son of God, who has eyes like a flame of fire, and His feet like fine brass: "I know your works, love, service, faith, and your patience; and as for your works, the last are more than the first. Nevertheless I have a few things against you, because you allow that woman Jezebel, who calls herself a prophetess, to teach and seduce My servants to commit sexual immorality and eat things sacrificed to idols. And I gave her time to repent of her sexual immorality, and she did not repent. Indeed I will cast her into a sickbed, and those who commit adultery with her into great tribulation, unless they repent of their deeds. I will kill her children with death, and all the churches shall know that I am He who searches the minds and hearts. And I will give to each one of you according to your works. "Now to you I say, and to the rest in Thyatira, as many as do not have this doctrine, who have not known the depths of Satan, as they say, I will put on you no other burden. But hold fast what you have till I come. And he who overcomes, and keeps My works until the end, to him I will give power over the nations— 'He shall rule them with a rod of iron;. They shall be dashed to pieces like the potter's vessels'— as I also have received from My Father; and I will give him the morning star.

He who has an ear, let him hear what the Spirit says to the churches.

Chapter Four - Hard is what makes it great

Do you remember the movie from a few years ago called
A League of Their Own? It was a film based on the All-
American Girls' Professional Baseball League, the league
formed in 1943 in an attempt to keep baseball in the
public eye after World War II reached America. In one of
the most powerful scenes in the movie, the star catcher of
the Rockford Peaches, Dottie Hinson, threatens to quit
the team. She's tired, she's worn out, she's worried about
her husband who has gone to war, and, in a low moment,
she is ready to walk away and throw in the towel. The
team manager, Jimmy Dugan, a former major league star,
tries to talk Dottie out of quitting. He says, "(Baseball) is

suppose to be hard... If it wasn't hard, everybody would do it!" And then he adds, *"Hard is what makes it great!"*

Some who have been walking with Christ for awhile understand that there are things about the Christian life that are hard as well. Nothing that would ever make you want to throw in the towel and quit, maybe, but certainly difficult, unpopular, uncomfortable choices that we are called to make along the path. Some having walked the Christian road for some time might say the same thing about the faith that Jimmy Dugan said about baseball, hard is one of the things that makes it great. In fact, the very root of the word "disciple" suggests discipline, and experience teaches us that Christian discipleship is a challenging discipline. Discipline, by its very nature is uncomfortable and difficult, at least at first. Jesus said:

Enter by the narrow gate; for wide is the gate and broad is the way that leads to destruction, and there are many who go in by it. Because narrow is the gate and difficult is the way which leads to life, and there are few who find it. Matthew 7:13-14

It's not easy. It's a narrow and difficult way, and we have to make daily choices to stay on track. Sometimes the footing is tricky because there is an enemy lurking in the shadows who will do anything to get you off the path. Not that slipping from the path causes us to lose our salvation or requires us to go back and start over, like a board game. It's more in the sense that we don't want to disappoint Him who died for our sins and are frustrated with ourselves when we feel like we have. I want to walk in the Spirit and not be driven by the flesh.

I don't believe Satan really thinks that he will be able to trick most of us into committing some grievous sin that will cause our faith to crash and burn, though it probably happens. Instead of a major blow-out, if he can just convince you to lower your standards, ease up on your morals, become more inclusive and tolerant, with a "what happens in Vegas stays in Vegas" mentality, then he's got you in a place called compromise, and that's right where he wants to keep you. You may still be saved, but you'll be worthless in battle, ineffective in advancing the kingdom. No threat to snatch others out of the fire and into God's peace. That, I believe, is the place the devil wants to get the church, to the land of spiritual compromise and deadness.

Union monopoly

Which brings us to the little town of Thyatira. It was difficult to live your faith in a public way in Thyatira because of the unusual pressure the community exerted upon its residents. Thyatira had been monopolized by unions, or worker fraternities, that controlled much of the commerce and employment in the region, which isn't bad in and of itself, but these unions were extremely fraternal, in an almost religious sort of way . They would sponsor activities and gathering that were religious, yet anti-Christian, including sex-based events at pagan temples or lavish meals including food that had been offered in sacrifice to idols, drunken parties and other events, many representing things that God had called the believers away from and that were now not a part of their lives in any way as they followed Christ.

William Barclay, the noted British scholar, wrote this about the unions of Thyatira:

"These guilds (unions) met frequently, and they met for a common meal. Such a meal was, at least in part, a religious ceremony. (They) would probably meet in a heathen temple, and it would certainly begin with a libation to the gods, and the meal itself would largely consist of meat offered to idols..."

The Christians rejected these indulgent, pagan, religious events. They wanted no part of it. But since the unions controlled the workplace, to earn a living you needed to be a member. Only, due to the questionable activities, the Christians really couldn't be a part of them. To be a member of the union, but avoid offensive activities, would have been difficult, and, at the very least, meant guilt by association. You really couldn't win. Being a Christian in Thyatira meant that you were asking for a life of trouble, because earning a living outside the unions would be hard, and working within the unions, while protecting your witness, would be even harder.

What would the answer be for the believers in this case? Leave? Go somewhere with a more acceptable work environment? Relax your standards and try to work in the anti-Christian environment? Stand firm in your beliefs and try to make a living outside of the worker guilds? No easy answers. So Jesus writes a letter to the church in Thyatira and to the people through the ages, maybe some people reading these words, to let us know He is mindful of every detail of our lives and trials.

The Son of God

These things says the Son of God, who has eyes like a flame of fire, and His feet like fine brass:

"These things says the Son of God." This is Jesus' only reference to Himself as the Son of God in Revelation. The church in Thyatira was going to receive some pretty stern directives in this letter, so Jesus begins by reminding them who is writing - **The Son of God.** This letter isn't from the old apostle John even though he had been the scribe Jesus used, it is from the Lord. He wanted them (and us) to know that right up front.

He who has eyes like fire and feet like brass. This speaks of His purity, truth and justice. He refines, burns to the core, roots out all impurity. The deity of Christ is not simply a doctrinal truth that we believe, it is the hinge pin of all creation. The fact that God would take on human form; become one of us, a man, a human being. Live a human life from birth through death, emotions to imagination, hurt to happiness, pleasure and pain, deal with everything we deal with (and much more). He was crucified for our sins and died on the cross of Calvary. He was buried in a tomb and conquered death by rising again, alive, on the third day, making a way, the only way, for us to be saved. John wrote:

And we know that the Son of God is come, and hath given us an understanding, that we may know him that is true, and we are in him that is true, [even] in his Son Jesus Christ. This is the true God, and eternal life. 1 John 5:20

Jesus is the Son of God, He is the true God, and eternal life.This truth was so critical to receiving the new life Christ offered, that understanding it was the purpose of John's entire gospel.

But these are written, that ye might believe that Jesus is the Christ, the Son of God; and that believing ye might have life through his name. John 20:31

When Paul wrote to the Galatian Christians, people who were being tempted to incorporate their former Jewish religious practices into the faith, he brought them back to this central, empowering reality:

I am crucified with Christ: nevertheless I live; yet not I, but Christ liveth in me: and the life which I now live in the flesh I live by the faith of the Son of God, who loved me, and gave himself for me. Galatians 2:20

Jesus is the Christ, the Son of the Living God. It is not a snappy mantra; it is the most liberating reality of all time. Believing in Christ sets us free from religion and Jesus wants the truth of His deity to be planted freshly and firmly in the forefront of our mind as He begins the letter because:

...there is no creature hidden from His sight, but all things are naked and open to the eyes of Him to whom we must give account. Hebrews 4:13

A well-oiled machine

I know your works, love, service, faith, and your patience; and as for your works, the last are more than the first.

If we would have visited a church service there in Thyatira, I'm certain that we would have been impressed, even amazed, at all the activity. Here was a group that had "church" figured out. In modern terminology, they would have had the bus ministry, the Sunday School, the recovery ministry, singles, MOPS, youth and everything else - all positive, solid ministries. Their calendar looked like a CPA at tax time - they were busy! And they just kept getting busier, the last works were more than the first, but activity is not what the Lord is looking for. What He wants first and foremost is our affection. Remember that Jesus said to "come unto Me" before He commissioned us to "go into all the world."

Nevertheless I have a few things against you, because you allow that woman Jezebel, who calls herself a prophetess, to teach and seduce My servants to commit sexual immorality and eat things sacrificed to idols.

Jesus refers to a woman in the church as Jezebel, in reference to the wife of King Ahab in the Old Testament. Jezebel was a wicked person who selfishly misled the children of Israel. The same spirit of Jezebel was at work in this woman in the Thyatira church, as well. She had a teaching platform of some kind and was leading people into idolatry and immorality. In the context of Thyatira's work environment, which was run by unions that expected members to participate in these very same kinds of activities, you can imagine what Jezebel might be teaching in the church:

The flesh and the spirit are separate. Things of the world, your work, what you eat, how you satisfy the urges of the flesh, these are worldly, fleshly appetites. Whereas the spirit, the inner man, is that part which is saved, sanctified, and glorified with Christ. They don't mix. Don't worry about what you do in the world, what is served for meat at the office parties, sexual liaisons that are a part of doing business, and the like, that's the flesh, it's of the world, it doesn't matter, it's separate from your spiritual life. Behavior doesn't matter.

And she may go further - *Actually, participating in these activities may enhance your witness because your fellow workers will see that you are not a straight-laced nut who doesn't know how to have fun. Being able to relate with them on a fleshly level may give you a chance to connect with them on a spiritual level. The end justifies the means.*

The practice of taking verses out of context to support points of our own invention is a powerful teaching method that many through the years have fallen victim to. The pattern is to cherry-pick verses from the Bible that appear to support what you want to say. Take a verse like 1 Corinthians 9:22:

"I am becoming all things to all men, that I might be able to win some"

In Thyatira, a scriptural concept like this could be twisted to mean that compromise in my conduct (becoming all things) is justifiable if my goal is to win people to Christ. Since the church in Thyatira was composed of people who were heavy on activity and light on spirituality, twisted scripture would have been easy to sneak into the community.

In our generation, a watered down version of the Gospel has resurfaced, not with the gnostic, separation of flesh and spirit doctrines so much, but the idea that, once you are saved, God overlooks what you do, think or say and behavior doesn't matter. So we fashion a gospel to fit our circumstances, one that disregards sinful behavior, showers us with grace when we ignore clearly defined biblical standards of conduct and lifestyle. Out of vogue and archaic are the concepts of holiness, sanctification and the cost of discipleship.

Greg Laurie asks the insightful question: *"In our zeal to acquaint Christians in the 90's with God's attributes of mercy, forgiveness and love for sinners, have we gone overboard? Why is there not more emphasis on God's attributes of holiness, righteousness and hatred for sin? Could it be that in our desire to become user-friendly, the church has compromised?"* (The Great Compromise)

God's standard is not adjustable, it's fixed. His law is not negotiable or open to debate. The spirit, soul and body are connected and whatever is inside our heart will be manifest through our conduct, for good or for ill.

"Brood of vipers! How can you, being evil, speak good things? For out of the abundance of the heart the mouth speaks." Matthew 12:34

A spiritual person that feeds deeply from the Word of God will not tolerate compromise in their lives, but be careful and conscious of their witness before men, striving to be a Christlike steward of God's grace and love.

So the Son of God says to wake up and recognize this spirit of compromise that is rampant in their midst.

Time to repent

And I gave her time to repent of her sexual immorality, and she did not repent.

One of the problems with false teaching is how people seem to get away with error. God doesn't appear to step in with judgement, so, it could appear that He actually approves of the doctrine, activity or lifestyle. Many false teachers seem actually to prosper, their error being celebrated, making people wonder if they might truly be blessed of God. But God is longsuffering, He is giving them time, but not because He approves; or He doesn't care, it's not because He is oblivious or powerless. The time He allows is time to repent, correct their course. He loves us, He loves His body. He loves those that are currently missing it or serving Him for the wrong reasons. He wants them to come around to the simplicity of the Gospel of Jesus Christ and repent. Just as He gave time to Jezebel to repent, but she did not repent.

The church in the tribulation

Indeed I will cast her into a sickbed, and those who commit adultery with her into great tribulation, unless they repent of their deeds. I will kill her children with death, and all the churches shall know that I am He who searches the minds and hearts. And I will give to each one of you according to your works.

Jezebel will reap what she has sown. Jesus is jealous for His bride, the church, and He won't allow misguided shepherds to lead it astray unchecked. So He writes this letter, both to Thyatira, who dealt with the issue of compromise late in the first century, and to the rest of us who battle it in our own age.

Some people wonder if the church will go through the Great Tribulation, and the answer is right there - *yes*. The unrepentant, compromising church, the church with the spirit of Jezebel that is no different from the world, full of idolatry and sexual immorality, cultivating no personal relationship with Jesus Christ, will be cast into great tribulation. Crystal clear. Does that mean the entire church living in the last days will go through the Great Tribulation period? It doesn't say that at all.

Just hang in there

Now to you I say, and to the rest in Thyatira, as many as do not have this doctrine, who have not known the depths of Satan, as they say, I will put on you no other burden. But hold fast what you have till I come.

What a wonderful assurance to the faithful. To those who resist compromise and stand firm in their faith, He says, just hold fast what you have till I come, I will put on you no other burden. Jesus knows that life is difficult for the Christians in Thyatira. Living there as a Christian would be a constant battle. Jesus knows that it is hard sometimes to maintain your holiness and purity and honesty and integrity, especially when the prevailing church culture says it's okay to fudge. But you hang in there because you know it brings honor to your Lord. And He says, "Just hold fast till I come."

And he who overcomes, and keeps My works until the end, to him I will give power over the nations - He shall rule them with a rod of iron. They shall be dashed to pieces like the potter's vessels'— as I also have received from My Father; and I will give him the morning star. He who has an ear, let him hear what the Spirit says to the churches.

After Jesus' second coming, there will be a time that the Bible describes as the millennium, a period of one thousand years, when Jesus will rule the world in righteousness. The promise here is that His faithful church, the faithful from Thyatira and all the rest through the ages, will rule with Christ.

There is another beautiful promise tucked into this final message to Thyatira, as well. In the book of Malachai, there is a prophesy that likens the second coming of Christ to the sunrise in the morning. It says:

"the Sun of Righteousness will arise with healing in His wings" (Malachai 4:2).

When Jesus returns it will be like the sunrise expelling the darkness and filling the earth with the brightness of His coming. No one will miss it, every eye will see, and everyone will know that He is Lord. But just before the sunrise, while it is still dark and the earth is still asleep, there shines the morning star for those up early enough to see it. In Revelation 22:16, Jesus calls himself the "bright morning star," and the subtle and beautiful picture here is of the rapture, or the "catching away," of the church prior to the second coming.

The faithful here in Thyatira, and the faithful in the church through the ages will *receive the bright morning star from Jesus*, He will come, just before the end of the age, and collect His church out of the earth, just as the wrath of God is unleashed on the world, and a short time before the sunrise of His second coming.

But we, like the Christians in Thyatira, need first to address this issue of compromise. Are there areas in your life where you have let your edge become dull? If you are a leader, have you led your church into the paths of righteousness and holiness for His glory? Or are you leading them into compromise through lack of discipleship, training and a personal lifestyle that models accommodation with the world? Are we slowly allowing the things of the world to infiltrate our ranks as harmless fun? Things like gambling, promiscuity, bad language, abortion, adultery, things that God instructs us both specifically and in principle to avoid? I often feel these things encroaching on my life, looking for a foothold, and I see it happening around me. We've got to stand strong, we've got to hold tight to the cross and hold fast till He comes.

Working from the inside out

As we close this letter, let me share a story I read about a certain 400 year old redwood tree. This old tree had survived four centuries in one of America's oldest forests. It had lived through fourteen separate lightning strikes. It had survived countless earthquakes, storms, floods, and other violent natural disasters. Yet one day, without warning, this massive, towering redwood came crashing to the ground. Dead. No bolt of lightning had triggered the fall, no overzealous lumberjack had sawn it down, it just fell, for no apparent reason. On closer examination, investigators discovered what finally conquered the old tree. Tiny beetles had found their way inside its trunk and had begun eating away at its fibers, weakening its enormous bulk. Imagine - what lightning bolts, storms and earthquakes could not do was easily accomplished over the passage of time by a handful of tiny insects working from the inside out.

It's the same with compromise. It's the little things that we justify, that we overlook, that get inside and dull our integrity and character. This is how the enemy will beat us. So the Lord gives us time, *this* time, to repent. Will you join me?

To the angel of the church in Sardis write,

These things says He who has the seven Spirits of God and the seven stars: "I know your works, that you have a name that you are alive, but you are dead. Be watchful, and strengthen the things which remain, that are ready to die, for I have not found your works perfect before God. Remember therefore how you have received and heard; hold fast and repent. Therefore if you will not watch, I will come upon you as a thief, and you will not know what hour I will come upon you. You have a few names even in Sardis who have not defiled their garments; and they shall walk with Me in white, for they are worthy. He who overcomes shall be clothed in white garments, and I will not blot out his name from the Book of Life; but I will confess his name before My Father and before His angels.

He who has an ear, let him hear what the Spirit says to the churches.

Chapter Five - Living in the Past

Sardis was known as one of the greatest cities in the world. In our day, it would be on par with places like New York City, London or Hong Kong. Geographically, Sardis was imposing. It was built on a mountain ridge nearly 1500 feet above the valley floor and was considered to be virtually impregnable. But twice in its history, against all odds, this seemingly invincible fortress had been attacked and overthrown, once by the Persians and again by the Greeks. Both successful conquests were achieved, not by traditional confrontation, but through stealth, as brave soldiers scaled the steep walls at night, entering lightly-guarded gates, laying siege to a sleeping city.

Unguarded, complacent, not as invincible as they thought they were or as formidable as they were thought to be. That was the story of the great city of Sardis. Unfortunately, the church in Sardis seemed to reflect their cities ongoing complacency. Churches do that. We tend to become, in some ways, like the communities we serve, reflecting the mores of the community, or country at large.

Weighed in the balance

These things says He who has the seven Spirits of God and the seven stars:

Remember those scales in old gold rush movies where the crusty miners would bring their bags of nuggets to be weighed and valued. It was an intricate contraption; platters on either side, a central standard, and delicate workings underneath. The little pile of shiny rocks would be placed on one side and the standard of measurement, placed on the other. The nuggets would be weighed in the balance and the true mass determined.

This picture of Jesus with the fullness of the Spirit in one hand, and the ministers of the church (see Revelation 1:20) in the other, gives us this image of a scale and suggests that the church is being weighed in this fashion. But contrary to what we might think, we are not being measured against other people or groups of believers (churches). The measuring standard is the fulness of the Spirit of Jesus Christ. As Paul wrote to the Ephesians:

Till we all come in the unity of the faith, and of the knowledge of the Son of God, unto a perfect man, unto the measure of the stature of the fulness of Christ: Ephesians 4:13

The measure is the stature of the fulness of Christ. In the prophecy of Isaiah, the Spirit of the Lord is described as resting upon the Christ, the Messiah, in its fulness:

The Spirit of the LORD shall rest upon Him, The Spirit of wisdom and understanding, The Spirit of counsel and might, The Spirit of knowledge and of the fear of the LORD. Isaiah 11:2

That's the measure of Christ's stature, the fulness of the Spirit of God. How does the church measure up to that standard? On the surface we fall short, right? Can we attain such a height? No, not in a million years in our own strength or goodness, to be sure. But, fortunately, we are not clothed in our own righteousness. Our righteousness is based on Christ's finished work. As we abide in Him, His fulness covers our emptiness; His plenty covers our lack and we can be weighed and found

Shining on the light of a brilliant past

I know your works, that you have a name that you are alive, but you are dead.

I read that light from the Polar Star takes thirty-three years to reach the earth. A reality like that is hard for my simple mind to grasp. I guess that means that the star could have imploded into darkness thirty years ago and yet its light would still be pouring down to earth. It would be shining tonight as brightly as if nothing had happened. It could be a dead star, shining solely on the light of a brilliant past.

That might describe the city of Sardis pretty well. Living on past glory, oblivious to present reality. Actually, that may describe some of us, as well. I used to tell a story of a summer that I baptized 100 people. I used the story as a teaching illustration about evangelism until I was struck by the conviction which said, essentially, "So what are you doing lately?"

Living in the past creates an unrealistic view of the present, it creates a false sense of security and confidence that today's challenges can be fixed by yesterday's success stories. But they can't. Today's hurts need fresh salve, not yesterdays story. There are real issues and needs going on right now that can't be fixed with last years brilliance. We need fresh life today. Unless the love of God is flowing through our lives - unless it is genuine, fresh, alive, powerful and current, we will be ineffectual in the world of today. Living in the past is just living in a dream world.

When you gonna wake up

Be watchful, ("wake up" NIV) and strengthen the things which remain, that are ready to die, for I have not found your works perfect before God.

There was a commercial on television, back in the 70's I think, for "Skin Bracer" after shave. It was some kind of distressed military conflict where a junior officer rushes over to the dozing commander and slaps him across the face with a handful of Skin Bracer and cries, *"Snap out of it, Sir!"* That's the image here, "Snap out of it! Wake up before it's too late!"

Bob Dylan wrote a song that was a charge to heed this exact advice. He wrote, in part:

"Do you ever wonder just what God requires? You think He's just an errand boy to satisfy your wandering desires? When you gonna wake up, strengthen the things that remain. God don't make promises that he don't keep. You got some big dreams baby but in order to dream you gotta still be asleep. When you gonna wake up, strengthen the things that remain."

It is hard to get the attention of someone who is daydreaming because daydreaming is such a pleasant escape from reality. Reality is hard and uncomfortable and never all about you. Jesus wants us to think about the past, but only to the extent that we remember what a living personal relationship with Him was like and get back there through repentance.

Remember therefore how you have received and heard; hold fast and repent.

Here's what the waking up process looks like.

First, *remember how you received the message,* remember your new birth in Christ. Do you recall the moment you came to Him by faith and experienced God's forgiveness, felt the shackles of guilt and shame leave you and felt God's love and mercy wash over your life like a flood? For some people, that was the only time you really encountered the Lord, you've never had another personal experience with Christ's touch. And that movement of God upon your life at salvation has become a monument that you vaguely recall, yet fondly remember. You have forgotten the vitality and excitement of those early days. Jesus says, "Remember."

This would be a good exercise for churches, as well, for most churches were born in a season of revival and would do well to just re-read their own heritage and seek the face of God for renewal and restoration.

Therefore if you will not watch, I will come upon you as a thief, and you will not know what hour I will come upon you.

Here is the word of warning. Jesus is very clear that the choice belongs to us. We have the ability to snap out of our slumber and repent, strengthening and renewing the relationship we once enjoyed. But if we choose not to, if we choose the past over the future and refuse to receive this word in the areas in which it applies, then here is what will happen; "I will come upon you as a thief, and you will not know what hour I will come upon thee."

This is a reference to Jesus' return which He described in a similar way to His disciples:

Then two men will be in the field: one will be taken and the other left. Two women will be grinding at the mill: one will be taken and the other left. Watch therefore, for you do not know what hour your Lord is coming. But know this, that if the master of the house had known what hour the thief would come, he would have watched and not allowed his house to be broken into. Therefore you also be ready, for the Son of Man is coming at an hour you do not expect. Matthew 24:40-44

Notice in verse 43 that this is how the coming of the Lord Jesus will begin, like a thief in the night. The idea that a thief would come in while you sleep, taking what he wants, then disappearing again into the night, gives us the feeling of helplessness. But if the homeowner would have known beforehand that the thief was coming, now that is a different story. With knowledge comes the power to be prepared. Jesus wants us to wake up and be watchful, not out of fear, but more out of longing for the fulfillment of His plan and certain return.

Behold, I tell you a mystery: We shall not all sleep, but we shall all be changed — in a moment, in the twinkling of an eye, at the last trumpet. For the trumpet will sound, and the dead will be raised incorruptible, and we shall be changed. I Corinthians 15:51-52

For the Lord Himself will descend from heaven with a shout, with the voice of an archangel, and with the trumpet of God. And the dead in Christ will rise first. Then we who are alive and remain shall be caught up together with them in the clouds to meet the Lord in the air. And thus we shall always be with the Lord. I Thessalonians 4:16-17

One day Jesus will come for His treasure, calling His bride from the four corners of the world, lifting us to spend eternity with Him. He will snatch us out of the world like a thief snatches the treasure out of a house. But it doesn't have to be a great surprise. Even though we do not know the day or the hour, we don't have to be overtaken as by a thief in the night. If we live with a sense of expectancy and in communion with Christ by His Spirit, we will always be ready for His return.

But concerning the times and the seasons, brethren, you have no need that I should write to you. For you yourselves know perfectly that the day of the Lord so comes as a thief in the night. For when they say, "Peace and safety!" then sudden destruction comes upon them, as labor pains upon a pregnant woman. And they shall not escape. But you, brethren, are not in darkness, so that this Day should overtake you as a thief. You are all sons of light and sons of the day. We are not of the night nor of darkness. Therefore let us not sleep, as others do, but let us watch and be sober. For those who sleep, sleep at night, and those who get drunk are drunk at night. But let us who are of the day be sober, putting on the breastplate of faith and love, and as a helmet the hope of salvation. For God did not appoint us to wrath, but to obtain salvation through our Lord Jesus Christ, who died for us, that whether we wake or sleep, we should live together with Him. Therefore comfort each other and edify one another, just as you also are doing. I Thessalonians 5:1-11

When the Lord comes to receive those who are His own, the people who are not watching, who are living only on past successes - asleep, if you will, and, the dead churches like Sardis with no light, no love and no power, will not be ready for Him. They will realize that they stayed in dreamland one day too long when they are overtaken as by a thief in the night. What will this look like, in terms of salvation and reward in heaven? I have no idea. But it is certain that those who are sober and watching and living in a personal, intimate relationship with Christ, will not be surprised and overtaken as by a thief.

The certainty of the certainty of His return excites the hearts of those who know our soon coming King personally and intimately. And hopefully, these words will stir the hearts of those who are dozing, complacent and living on past glory.

He's coming soon

There are so many people who, while they believe in the second coming of Christ, deep down in their hearts don't believe He will come any time soon. Do you fall in to that camp? It's okay if you do, it's pretty natural, actually. But some folks actually bristle at the thought of guys like me, scaring the beans out of people with the message of the second coming and the rapture of the church and the season of great tribulation.

"The nerve of those religious wackos!" they'll say. But the message doesn't need to be housed in spooky, theological garb that no one fully understands. Neither myself or anyone else knows when Jesus is coming back and it could be in a million years, nobody knows but our Heavenly Father. But that doesn't mean we don't have to deal with it, because the truth is that one way or another, Jesus is coming *for you* very soon. His personal return might not take place for awhile but one thing, to which everyone can attest, is that each of us will eventually die. No *body* lives forever.

Death, as they say, is a fact of life. And, for the most part, it comes upon us in some unexpected fashion. You never really know from one day to the next what life will hold, this really could be your (or my) last day on earth. That's not a pessimistic fatalist view, that's just reality, and we all live it every day. Now, putting aside the fact that Jesus will personally come again, every day He receives children to their heavenly home. Those who are sick, those who are victims of some kind of tragedy or disease - people die every day. For those who are alive with Christ, that moment doesn't come like a thief in the night - it comes as an expected, even welcome part of life. Christians look forward to heaven, they don't dread it. While for those outside of Christ, death comes like a thief.

So will Jesus return in our generation? Well, in the sense that every person in our generation will return to Him, yes. Because while He may or may not make His second coming as the King of Kings and Lord of Lords to rule and reign for a millennium, He definitely will come for each of us individually for

"... man is destined to die once, and after that to face judgment" Hebrews 9:27.

The exhortation here is to be ready, be awake, be watchful - and that day will not overtake you as a thief.

You have a few names even in Sardis who have not defiled their garments; and they shall walk with Me in white, for they are worthy. He who overcomes shall be clothed in white garments, and I will not blot out his name from the Book of Life; but I will confess his name before My Father and before His angels. He who has an ear, let him hear what the Spirit says to the churches.

Come now, and let us reason together, Says the LORD, Though your sins are like scarlet, They shall be as white as snow; Though they are red like crimson, They shall be as wool. Isaiah 1:18

That is what the blood of the Lamb of God does with the overcomers - it makes them white like snow, cleansed and righteous. We aren't worthy to be clothed in white because we are better than anybody else. We are worthy because of Jesus, because of what He has done, not by any righteous works of our own. We are not earning our way to heaven, we could never pay that price. We are just believing His word and trusting in His cleansing blood to wash away our sins. All of the people in the world from the youngest to the oldest, from the poorest to the most wealthy, all those with a simple faith in Christ, will be dressed in white in heaven. It's not based on what we did in the past, it's not based on what we'll do in the future, it's because of Jesus Christ, the Way, the Truth and the Life. That white robe He wraps around us is the righteousness of Jesus Christ. We are all clothed in His finished work, not our own.

What about my salvation?

Some folks really struggle with the statement Jesus makes here in the letter to Sardis, "And I will not blot out his name out of the book of life," and they wonder, "Does this mean I can lose my salvation?" "Does this verse imply that God has a heavenly eraser and He actually blots out names?!" And the answer is, I don't know.

How's that for confident pastoral wisdom? But notice, He doesn't say anyone's name is being blotted out. Rather, Jesus is reassuring them that those who overcome and trust Him never have to worry about that! *Ever.* That's good news. That's great news! Instead, He says he will acknowledge you before His Father and before the angels.

Right where you belong

Have you ever walked in to a party and felt completely out of place? We have this fear that we will arrive at a gathering and people will look at us like we have corn stalks growing out of our ears, like we are in the wrong place and no one wants us there. I was at a party one time for the Grammy Awards and felt like this. Lots of celebrities and musicians and industry big-shots were there, milling around, laughing and schmoozing, and in we walk. I was surprised to be on the guest list at all, sort of expecting for the people at the door to say, "Oh, we're sorry Mr. Gobble, (as it is often mispronounced) you aren't on the list." It was so uncomfortable to be in the room that I thought I'd just graze around the buffet table for a few minutes and get out of there while my pride was still intact. Then one of the senior guys from the record company sees me from across the room, and comes over smiling and seemingly happy to see me. He took a minute to introduce me to a few people and I began to feel safe, like maybe I did belong.

And Jesus will do the same thing for us in heaven. You won't wander around for long before He spots you, and His eyes will light up and He'll be so excited, because the extra special person that He came to earth for, the one He walked with through all those uniquely difficult trials and tribulations known only to you and Him, is finally home. He will run to you and embrace you and introduce you to His Father and the angels as His child and friend. And you will know that you are at home. Safe. Right where you are supposed to be, home where you belong.

Keep your torch lit till the end

In ancient Greece, they had a race in their Olympic games that was unique in that the runners all carried torches. The winner was the runner who finished with his torch still lit. Everyone started with a flame, but not all finished with the fire still burning. Starting is important, starting is critical, but finishing with the torch still lit is imperative.

What really matters is not just the fact that your torch for Christ was lit at one time, but the fact that it stays lit through thick and thin, all the way to the end of the race.

Don't live in the light of the past, Jesus wants to ignite your life right now and do something in and through you that you might not believe even if He told you about it. Wake up, get ready and run back to Jesus.

And to the angel of the church in Philadelphia write,

These things says He who is holy, He who is true, "He who has the key of David, He who opens and no one shuts, and shuts and no one opens": "I know your works. See, I have set before you an open door, and no one can shut it; for you have a little strength, have kept My word, and have not denied My name. Indeed I will make those of the synagogue of Satan, who say they are Jews and are not, but lie—indeed I will make them come and worship before your feet, and to know that I have loved you. Because you have kept My command to persevere, I also will keep you from the hour of trial which shall come upon the whole world, to test those who dwell on the earth. Behold, I am coming quickly! Hold fast what you have, that no one may take your crown. He who overcomes, I will make him a pillar in the temple of My God, and he shall go out no more. I will write on him the name of My God and the name of the city of My God, the New Jerusalem, which comes down out of heaven from My God. And I will write on him My new name.

He who has an ear, let him hear what the Spirit says to the churches.

Chapter Six - Faithful

I remember talking to my friends Bernie and Sue about trust in their marriage. Sue really believed that it was just a matter of time until her husband proved unfaithful. Infidelity was everywhere; celebrities, television, even her own parents marriage had been shipwrecked by adultery. She was worried that her own marriage would be a casualty as well, if not soon then certainly eventually.

But Bernie wasn't unfaithful, in fact, he was the most devoted, loving husband a woman could hoped for. Actually, he was exactly the kind of man Sue needed, one that could demonstrate faithfulness and love to her so that she could be delivered from fear and healed. My message to them was simple:

"Faithfulness isn't a short-term virtue. It may take a lifetime, but over the process of God making one out of the two of you, daily, regular, persevering faithfulness will bring healing and trust to your marriage."

Wounded by adultery and divorce, popular culture and personal insecurity would not permit her wound to heal. The prescription for healing would be a combination of faithfulness and time. Not one or the other, but both, experienced daily, administered prayerfully by a loving husband who was going to be there for the long haul. They break new ground in their relationship every day as they discover the power of faithfulness.

The church at Philadelphia is kind of like Sue's loving husband Bernie. They made the commitment to be faithful, and this letter from Jesus is a commendation for that faithfulness. It's a great lesson for us as we read how they did it and what Jesus has in store for his faithful ones through the ages. He begins with a description of Himself that is fresh and different from the picture He has given in the other letters.

These things says He who is holy, He who is true, He who has the key of David, He who opens and no one shuts, and shuts and no one opens.

Jesus is holy and true. He is separated from sin, morally perfect, consecrated to God. Jesus lived a flesh and blood life, exactly like yours and mine, with the key differences being that He didn't bring a sinful nature into life, and He never committed sin. He was perfect in every moral, ethical, emotional way. He is separate and set apart from sin.

He is holy. We need to remember the holiness of Christ when we think of Him and speak of Him because there is a tendency to try to pull Him down to our level and buddy-up with Him. He bridged the great divide between God and man, becoming man, facing every temptation and trial we ever could, and more, and He did so without sin. His standard is higher than we could ever attain, everything good we could ever do would be like a pile of dirty rags in comparison to His slightest attribute. He is holy.

He is true. He not only has the name of truth, but it is His very nature, He is the truth. He is genuine, the opposite of what is counterfeit, imaginary or fictitious.

When Jesus speaks to the depth of your soul with a word of insight, it's as true as true can be. There is no question, no nuance, no shadow, *it's just true*. Because He is true.

Our response to His truth is to listen and obey because as the Holy and True one, His aim is our wholeness and His goal is our restoration and relationship. Our best interest is His sole intention so there is never a need to question or hesitate in our response. For Holy and True is who Jesus is.

He opens doors that no one can shut

He opens doors that no one can shut and shuts doors that no one can open. If He opens it, it is open before you. And if He has closed the door, there is no use looking for a key. There will be no getting in. This is a beautiful image that I pray over people daily.

The reference here is to a passage in Isaiah where God is replacing the operations man at the temple because he has been running some kind of dupe for his own gain. God says He's going to whirl around and shot-put the guy into another country and replace him with a godly man, Eliakim, of whom the Lord says:

The key of the house of David I will lay on his shoulder; So he shall open, and no one shall shut; And he shall shut, and no one shall open. I will fasten him as a peg in a secure place, And he will become a glorious throne to his father's house. Isaiah 11:22-23

In other words, Eliakim would hold the keys to the treasures and resources of the kingdom, and whatever he said would be the final word, a "yes," from Eliakim, was yes, and a "no" was no. What he says goes.

Here in the letter to the church in Philadelphia, Jesus applies this authority to Himself, declaring essentially that no power in heaven or earth, no human or heavenly authority can overrule or contravene His word. If He opens a door, it won't be shut, and if He shuts it, it can't be opened. Thank you Lord that You hold the keys!

He holds the keys

What a wonderful promise for those of us who are looking for direction in life and ministry. We can bring our requests confidently before the Lord knowing that He is holy and true, that he always has our best interest in mind, and that He has the ability to open doors of life, love and work in front of us. According to His will, we can ask that the doors be opened before us, and if they are opened by Him, they can't be shut! Amen!

On the other hand, if a door is shut, we don't have to fret and whine and search for another way of getting what we want, because He has shut the door. And that's okay. His will is for our good. I don't want to go through doors He has shut before me anyway! So knowing this about Jesus makes our faith journey and prayer so much clearer. If He opens the door, I proceed, and if He closes it, I don't.

I know your works. See, I have set before you an open door, and no one can shut it; for you have a little strength, have kept My word, and have not denied My name.

Jesus saw their works and opened a door for them that could not be shut. What a wonderful encouragement this would be for the readers of this letter. They are praying about some kind of need, a new mission field they want to enter, or a people group they desire to reach, whatever it was, and Jesus says, "I've seen what you are doing, and I have opened the door for you, *the answer is yes.*"

When we read this passage it's natural to do a quick mental review of the areas you have been praying for recently, like relationships, career, ministry, witnessing, and you ask the Lord, "Is this word for me?" "Are you opening a door in that area I have been praying about?" "Is my answer *yes*?" That's a reasonable question because God does use things as simple as this study to speak and confirm His word to your life. However, before you reach for the door knob, notice why Jesus has opened the door before this little church:

For you have a little strength, have kept My word, and have not denied My name.

He opens doors before the faithful. The open doors are set before those who are strong, even just a little, those who keep His word and do not deny His name.

A little strength

You don't have to be strong by any worldly measurement to be strong in the Lord. To be strong in the Lord is to walk honestly with Him by faith, holding nothing back in your allegiance and love. Paul draws a picture for us of putting on a suit of armor, with each piece of equipment representing an aspect of our walk with God and its ability to fit you for spiritual battle (Ephesians 6:11-18). If you and I and our churches just have enough strength to put on the armor, that's enough, for the battle belongs to the Lord. We need but a little strength.

Also, we must keep His word. Time and again, Jesus exhorted His disciples to keep His word. God's word is the key ingredient of our spiritual diet.

If you love Me, keep My commandments. John 14:15

He who has My commandments and keeps them, it is he who loves Me." And he who loves Me will be loved by My Father, and I will love him and manifest Myself to him. John 14:21

If you keep My commandments, you will abide in My love, just as I have kept My Father's commandments and abide in His love. John 15:10

Believing, knowing and obeying the things Jesus taught is so critical to our life and relationship with Him that He instructed the disciples to make His teachings the primary curriculum for the discipleship of new believers.

And Jesus came and spoke to them, saying, 'All authority has been given to Me in heaven and on

earth. Go therefore and make disciples of all the nations, baptizing them in the name of the Father and of the Son and of the Holy Spirit, teaching them to observe all things that I have commanded you; and lo, I am with you always,even to the end of the age.' Amen. Matthew 28:18-20

See it there? "Teaching them (the new disciples) to observe all the things I have commanded you." If we are ignorant of His commands, or careless with our attention to His instructions, why would we imagine that a door of opportunity or service would be opened before us. Keeping His word is a prerequisite to open doors.

And they did not deny His name. This is probably a bigger issue than it appears to be from the surface. Because it's easy to honor His name when surrounded by like-minded believers in a worship service. The hard part is honoring His name in the little things of life, the unremarkable deeds done for unappreciative people in unglamorous circumstances. These are the opportunities to honor or deny His name. Jesus put it like this:

Then the King will say to those on His right hand, 'Come, you blessed of My Father, inherit the kingdom prepared for you from the foundation of the world: for I was hungry and you gave Me food; I was thirsty and you gave Me drink; I was a stranger and you took Me in; I was naked and you clothed Me; I was sick and you visited Me; I was in prison and you came to Me. Then the righteous will answer Him, saying, 'Lord, when did we see You hungry and feed You, or thirsty and give You drink? When did we see You a stranger and take You in, or naked and clothe You? Or when did we see You sick, or in prison, and come to You?' And the King will answer and say to them, 'Assuredly, I say to you, inasmuch as you did it to one of the least of these My brethren, you did it to Me.' Matthew 25:34-40

The big and dramatic is easier by far than the discipline of dying to ourself daily in selfless service for Christ. But that is faithfulness. And that is what brought Jesus to Philadelphia with His keys to open a door before them.

Indeed I will make those of the synagogue of Satan, who say they are Jews and are not, but lie—indeed I will make them come and worship before your feet, and to know that I have loved you.

This is an fascinating reference to the Jews who were the physical but not the spiritual descendants of Abraham.

That is, they were not people of faith like Abraham was, they were just religious. Jesus minced no words with this group of Pharisees when he spoke to them declaring that they were not true descendants of Abraham but were instead of their "father the devil" (John 8:44). Now this is not to say that He does not love the Jews or receive each one who reaches out to Him in faith. On the contrary, Jesus came first for the children of Israel, the children of the promise, they were His top priority and primary aim. God longs for the time when many hundreds of thousands will realize that He is Messiah and return to Him in repentance and love, and He wants us to pray for that day as well (Psalm 122:6). But Jesus has no time for false religion. And false religion performed in His Father's name is doubly bad. So He just calls it what it is, a synagogue of Satan.

So Jesus begins to describe what is going to happen, or, more precisely, what He is going to orchestrate, and that is a time when the religious Jews will ultimately acknowledge Christ and His acceptance of the Gentiles. For many sincere Jewish men and women, that day has come, and they are following Christ as their promised Messiah. Praise the Lord!

Because you have kept My command to persevere, I also will keep you from the hour of trial which shall come upon the whole world, to test those who dwell on the earth.

Many commentators believe that this "hour of trial" is a reference to the Great Tribulation, the period of time at the end of the age when the wrath of God is poured out on a sinful world.

And at that time shall Michael stand up, the great prince which standeth for the children of thy people: and there shall be a time of trouble, such as never was since there was a nation [even] to that same time: Daniel 12:1a

For then shall be great tribulation, such as was not since the beginning of the world to this time, no, nor ever shall be. Matthew 24:21

And I will execute vengeance in anger and fury upon the heathen, such as they have not heard. Micah 5:15

During this season of Great Tribulation, God promises to deliver His people and spare them from His wrath, mentioning it here to the Philadelphian church, and elsewhere:

...and at that time thy people shall be delivered, every one that shall be found written in the book. Daniel 12:1b

Come, my people, enter your chambers, And shut your doors behind you; Hide yourself, as it were, for a little moment, Until the indignation is past. For behold, the LORD comes out of His place To punish the inhabitants of the earth for their iniquity; The earth will also disclose her blood, And will no more cover her slain. Isaiah 26:20-21

Watch ye therefore, and pray always, that ye may be accounted worthy to escape all these things that shall come to pass, and to stand before the Son of man. Luke 21:36

Escape; Delivered; "Kept from;" - these words speak of a commitment by God to somehow remove His church before the day of wrath arrives. Teachers call this event the rapture of the church, a phrase taken from the Greek word "harpazo" found in 1 Thessalonians 4:17.

"Then we who are alive and remain shall be caught up together with them in the clouds to meet the Lord in the air. And thus we shall always be with the Lord."

The phrase "caught up" in our English Bible, is the Greek word "harpazo" which means to "snatch away with force" - like a little boy might reach out and grab a lizard as it tries to scurry away. Harpazo translates into Latin as "raptus," where we get the English word, rapture.

There is some question as to the point at which the church will be raptured or caught away, mostly revolving around the understanding of the terms describing the Great Tribulation period, with some believing the whole seven-year period is the time of God's wrath and others holding the view that the last half of the tribulation is the time of God's wrath. But both agree that it is in the character of God and the teaching of scripture that God will deliver His own prior to pouring out His wrath as He demonstrated with Noah's family.

Firmly established forever

Behold, I am coming quickly! Hold fast what you have, that no one may take your crown. He who overcomes, I will make him a pillar in the temple of My God, and he shall go out no more. I will write on

him the name of My God and the name of the city of My God, the New Jerusalem, which comes down out of heaven from My God. And I will write on him My new name.

Philadelphia was a city that had been previously destroyed by earthquakes. People had been forced to flee the city numerous times after large quakes and intense aftershocks. This allusion of making the believers pillars in the temple of God gives me an interesting visual, not the humorous image of people holding up a building, but the image of an area after an earthquake, or a scene from ancient ruins, where just about the only things left standing after some type of devastation are the pillars of the buildings. Have you ever noticed that in pictures of ancient ruins? Pillars have a weight and permanence and strength about them that suggest the structure is something that will last forever. The promise here is that there would be no more running for cover, no more escape, but instead there would be a permanent place with God in His house, within His walls.

No more running. No more hiding. No more fight or flight. No running from people, running from problems, running for cover, ever again. Now, instead, we will stand as a pillars in God's house, firmly established, secure with

God's name emblazoned upon our life, standing under the banner of God's eternal city. What a great promise!

He who has an ear, let him hear what the Spirit says to the churches.

But as it is written: Eye has not seen, nor ear heard, Nor have entered into the heart of man The things which God has prepared for those who love Him. 1 Corinthians 2:9

And to the angel of the church of the Laodiceans write,

These things says the Amen, the Faithful and True Witness, the Beginning of the creation of God: "I know your works, that you are neither cold nor hot. I could wish you were cold or hot. So then, because you are lukewarm, and neither cold nor hot, I will vomit you out of My mouth. Because you say, 'I am rich, have become wealthy, and have need of nothing'—and do not know that you are wretched, miserable, poor, blind, and naked— I counsel you to buy from Me gold refined in the fire, that you may be rich; and white garments, that you may be clothed, that the shame of your nakedness may not be revealed; and anoint your eyes with eye salve, that you may see. As many as I love, I rebuke and chasten. Therefore be zealous and repent. Behold, I stand at the door and knock. If anyone hears My voice and opens the door, I will come in to him and dine with him, and he with Me. To him who overcomes I will grant to sit with Me on My throne, as I also overcame and sat down with My Father on His throne.

He who has an ear, let him hear what the Spirit says to the churches.

Chapter Seven - Lukewarm is never good

This letter is for people who believe their own press. Ouch, right? People with an estimation of their own greatness that eclipses reality. Many of us carry an appearance of humility while secretly harboring high feelings of our own importance and value. Just about everyone who experiences a measure of prosperity or success deals with this pride-based issue. Not everyone takes the bait, not everyone falls victim to his own success, but enough of us do that Jesus writes a letter to a church that had it made from every material angle. Yet His appraisal of their health was exactly the opposite of what appeared, and it alerts us to the very real need to keep our lives and resources in careful perspective in relation to God's will and purpose in the world.

Not what we have, but what has us

We aren't blessed with resources and material goods exclusively for our own benefit. The fact that some people are born into wealthy societies, and some in impoverished lands, some in peaceful regions, and others in war-torn countries, some with a "Midas touch" for wealth creation, and others who can never seem to scrape two dimes together, needs to remind us that this life has less to do with what we have and more to do with what has us. Less to do with how much we can accumulate and more to do with how much we can give.

These things says the Amen, the Faithful and True Witness, the Beginning of the creation of God:

Jesus begins by describing the unique position He holds from which He can provide an accurate account. *He is the beginning of the creation of God.* This places Him in the beginning with God, nothing has happened that precedes Him (John 1:3). Also, He lived in space and time, yet transcended it by rising again from the dead, alive forevermore. Therefore, His unique perspective takes every angle into account - past, present and future.

He is the faithful and true witness. In a courtroom, the faithful witness is the one who honestly reports "the truth, the whole truth, and nothing but the truth." He is faithful to reveal the whole truth about my life, good or bad. What He reports is the word of the faithful and true witness. He is the Amen - the final word, the bottom line, the end of the discussion. Paul writes:

For all the promises of God in Him are Yes, and in Him Amen, to the glory of God through us. 2 Corinthians 1:20

The writer of Hebrews explains:

God, who at various times and in various ways spoke in time past to the fathers by the prophets, has in these last days spoken to us by His Son, whom He has appointed heir of all things, through whom also He made the worlds. Hebrews 1:1,2

In the context of a report about the church and our lives, Jesus is God's answer, promise and final word.

I know your works, that you are neither cold nor hot. I could wish you were cold or hot. So then, because you are lukewarm, and neither cold nor hot, I will vomit you out of My mouth.

Sometimes we hear these verses preached from the perspective that God would rather have us on fire and full of zeal for Him, or totally against Him and cold toward His love, just not in between where we believe but don't change. And He makes it clear that lukewarm is not an option for the believer. But we might have the idea of hot and cold skewed a bit from His original intention. Because, while Jesus does want us to be a fully-devoted disciple, on fire for Him, if you will, he doesn't want anyone to be cold to His love. His desire is for everyone to be saved and come to repentance. He died for the whole world, He conquered sin, death and the grave for everyone, and He says "come to me all who are weary and heavy laden, and I will give you rest." I don't think he prefers that people be "cold" in the sense of relationship with Him, at all.

Instead, a hint at His intention, which might have been obvious to the people of Laodicea, is found in the community water supply. In a word, *they didn't have one.*

Fresh water

Laodicea didn't have a fresh water supply. This wealthy, upper-middle class city, that appeared to have everything, had to have their water piped in. Now, they were wealthy enough to arrange for that, which was good, but unlike neighboring towns, they had no fresh water supply of their own that regularly supplied the city. Barclay notes that Colossae, a city just a few miles away, had a crisp mountain spring that fed their community with fresh, cool spring water. Heirapolis, another regional community, had the benefit of a piping hot mineral springs bubbling up for their water supply, Laodicea had neither. So a water system was built to divert the precious resource into Laodicea. But, by the time water reached the city, it was stale, lukewarm and barely drinkable.

I think Jesus hits a soft spot when He says that He wished they were hot or cold, *anything but lukewarm*. These folks probably wished that every day when they went out to the well, "I wish this water was cold, like the spring in Colossae, or even hot, like the mineral water in Heirapolis. Cold or hot, anything but this!"

There was an old beverage commercial which had a tagline about "taking the Nestea Plunge." There would be some guy on a smoldering hot pool deck, parched and baking in the summer heat, and he picks up a tall, icy glass of tea, and the camera shifts into slow motion as he brings it to his lips and drinks the icy treat while simultaneously falling backwards into the refreshing pool, glass and all - the Nestea Plunge. Who wouldn't prefer to reach into a cooler full of frosty beverages and pull out an icy drink to quench your thirst, rather than drink from a half-empty plastic two-liter bottle that had been sitting on a picnic table in the hot sun for most of the day. Pretty simple. A lukewarm drink is not only stale and flavorless, it's nauseating and unsatisfying. Cold is refreshing.

The same goes for a hot cocoa or steaming cup of coffee on a cold morning. It's got to be hot. Lukewarm is almost never good.

Jesus would rather have a church that is either hot and zealous or cold and refreshing, just not lukewarm and stagnant. Lukewarm is not an option. "Well, they aren't impacting the community for Christ, but at least they show up and have church every Sunday." "We may be lukewarm, but at least we're here."

And Jesus says to the lukewarm, the one who is coasting, dozing, going through the motions, those who are stagnant, stale, and flavorless, you've got to be expelled, vomited out.

Self (mis)perception

Because you say, I am rich, have become wealthy, and have need of nothing — and do not know that you are wretched, miserable, poor, blind, and naked — I counsel you to buy from Me gold refined in the fire, that you may be rich; and white garments, that you may be clothed, that the shame of your nakedness may not be revealed; and anoint your eyes with eye salve, that you may see.

The reason for our lukewarmness is right here. We have an estimation of ourselves that is the opposite of reality. Jesus points to wealth, speaking to our pride, independence and self-sufficiency. Our actions suggest that we don't really need God, we have all we need. We are so tied to the physical realm that, if we prosper materially, we rock into a sense of security like a baby in a cradle. But it is false security. The truth is that security and success in life has very little if anything to do with material possessions. These things may be the worldly standard, but Jesus, the faithful and true witness, sees what we are really made of and says, "No, you aren't wealthy at all, honestly, you are wretched, miserable, poor, blind and naked."

Buy from Me

His counsel is that what we need in life comes from Him, "buy from Me..." is the key He offers. Not that we can purchase anything from God, or that He has anything for sale, the point is that everything that is needed for life and godliness is found in Christ. The gold tried in the fire represents our precious faith and the white robes are the righteousness of Christ. His healing touch that makes us whole, well and alive, enables us to see what is truly important. If we fail to see that our worth, value and inheritance is in Christ alone, then we are poor indeed.

As many as I love, I rebuke and chasten. Therefore be zealous and repent. Behold, I stand at the door and knock. If anyone hears My voice and opens the door, I will come in to him and dine with him, and he with Me.

If you are in a lukewarm, flavorless, stagnant place in your walk with Christ, this letter is written to remind you that Jesus loves you so much that He wants you to know the truth.

These verses are usually used at invitation time where Jesus is pictured knocking on the door of the unbelieving heart, asking them to open the door to His love. But the context of the letter is to Christians, entire churches, who have grown distant and stale in their relationship with Christ. While the message holds true for an invitation, it is all the more critical to be received by the sleeping, lukewarm Christian and the stagnant, lifeless church. Open the door to Jesus and let your value and vision be found in Him alone, not in your personal resources.

To him who overcomes I will grant to sit with Me on My throne, as I also overcame and sat down with My Father on His throne. He who has an ear, let him hear what the Spirit says to the churches.

This isn't an image of sitting on Santa's lap in the mall - this is a picture of rulership. Christ rules from the throne of God, and He invites the overcomer to sit with Him, reign with Him, and be part of His heavenly team.

Replacing the stagnant and stale with that which is refreshing and alive requires a transfusion of God's love. It requires a fresh filling of His Spirit and a fresh encounter with Jesus Christ. Andrew Murray wrote, *"May not a single moment of my life be spent outside the light, love and joy of God's presence and not a moment without the entire surrender of my self as a vessel for Him to fill full of His Spirit and His love."*

I think there are a lot of vessels that need a fresh filling today, a transfusion, if you will. If you will open the door to His grace and welcome the fullness of His Holy Spirit to flow into your life, times of refreshing will come from the presence of God. There is nothing magical about opening that door, but it is the only path of refreshing and life with the Lord.

And the Spirit and the Bride say, Come!" And let him who thirsts come. Whoever desires, let him take the water of life freely. Revelation 22:17

Conclusion

Seven is used in scripture in a number of ways (no pun intended,) among them, to convey completion and fullness (Genesis 2:1; Revelation 15:1). In Revelation 2 & 3, Jesus wrote seven letters that, from the surface, look somewhat limited in scope. They are addressed to specific groups of people, living and working at the end of the first century, written with very personal observations of the individuals involved and with exacting detail of the historical, cultural setting in which they lived.

With a closer look, we realize that these personal notes, addressed to other people and written 2000 years ago, also pinpoint details of our own lives that are sometimes too close, in their accuracy and bluntness, for comfort. As the sharp sword of the Word of God, Jesus cuts through space and time and writes letters that, at the same time, apply to every follower in every generation, the whole church, those who were, are, and those who are yet to come.

You were on His mind

When Jesus wrote these notes, He wasn't just thinking about the union worker in Thyatira, He was thinking about the Teamster in Billings, Montana. He wasn't just writing to the angel of the church in Ephesus, He was writing to the pastor of the church in Lexington. With this realization comes the potential for ongoing, very personal application of these truths to the Christian life. I wouldn't venture to guess the issues and situations these letters have applied to over the years; I've just tried to note a few, specific to me and you and our generation. But God's Spirit can, does and will reveal so much more to the individual with an open mind and a receptive heart, the person, as He says,

"with ears to hear what the Spirit is saying."

May God richly bless you.

Made in the USA
Lexington, KY
26 January 2013